Family Secrets

Addison-Wesley Publishing Company, Inc.

Reading, Massachusetts   Menlo Park, California   New York
Don Mills, Ontario   Wokingham, England   Amsterdam   Bonn
Sydney   Singapore   Tokyo   Madrid   San Juan
Paris   Seoul   Milan   Mexico City   Taipei

Family Secrets

*How Telling and Not Telling
Affect Our Children,
Our Relationships, and
Our Lives*

HARRIET WEBSTER

To protect the privacy of those who told me their stories, I have changed the names and places, and sometimes occupations or other identifying details. Each story, however, is a true one. There are no composites here.

Library of Congress Cataloging-in-Publication Data

Webster, Harriet.
    Family secrets : how telling and not telling affect our children, our relationships, and our lives / Harriet Webster.
        p.   cm.
    Includes bibliographical references.
    ISBN 0 201 19788 X
    ISBN 0 201 60012 X (pbk.)
    1. Family.   2. Secrecy—Psychological aspects.   3. Interpersonal relations.   I. Title.
HQ734.W414   1991
306.874—dc20   90-22828
                                                                      CIP

Cover design by Marjorie Anderson
Text design by Barbara Werden
Set in 11-point Sabon by Camden Type 'n Graphics
1 2 3 4 5 6 7 8 9-MW-95949392
First printing, March 1991
First paperback printing, March 1992

For my children, David, Matt, and Ben

Contents

Preface

Family Secrets is a book about the emotional fallout that often occurs when families keep secrets. It is about the intricate dance executed by parents and children, brothers and sisters, grandparents, aunts and uncles as they contrive to hide or deny a part of their own experience or the experiences of others in their family.

Many of us resort to secrecy when we feel threatened or ashamed. We turn to concealment as an obvious strategy for coping with incidents that we wish never happened. By banishing them to a dark corner, we save ourselves from dealing with the difficult, often painful feelings that disturbing incidents can provoke in us and our children.

Although all of these subjects are raised in the stories that follow, *Family Secrets* is not a book about clouded parentage or homosexuality, incest or mental illness. It is a book about the phenomenon of secrecy as it plays out in our families. The common thread that stitches the stories together is the consistent message that whatever the content of the secret, the damage would have been less if the issue had been brought out in the open, acknowledged, and confronted.

It appears to be the act of concealing, of putting a noose on the expression of feelings, that leads to the sense of distrust that plagues many who have experienced family secrets. The people I interviewed were united in their belief that no matter what happened, no matter how dreadful, shrouding the incident in secrecy only exacerbated the damage by creating an atmosphere of uncertainty and distrust, an atmosphere where feelings could not be expressed and respected. Their experiences illustrate the many ways secrecy can come into play within a family. They provide insight into helpful and harmful ways to deal with family secrets. Their reflections offer many suggestions as to how and when to convey sensitive information to children, as well as how to define the line between privacy and secrecy.

Because I am a journalist by trade, not a psychiatrist or a psychologist, I have chosen to approach my subject by collecting and telling stories which people have told to me as they explain how the phenomenon of secrecy has played out in their lives. I began all the interviews by asking my subjects what thoughts the word *secrecy* evoked in them when applied to their own families. As they related their tales, I continually asked how they felt about what had happened. I asked too how they would approach a similar issue with their own children.

I found my subjects through word of mouth. For two years, I told nearly everyone I met that I was writing a book about family secrets. I gave them some examples of the kinds of secrets I had come across. More often than not, the people I talked to either were reminded of some incident in their own families or they knew someone else who had grappled with a family secret. They sent me to their relatives, to people they had met through their work, to their neighbors, their piano teachers, their childhood friends. I would call these people, and most of them agreed to be interviewed. I met some of them in their homes, others after hours in their offices, a few in restaurants or parks. The interviews were loosely structured. Mostly, I wanted to hear their stories and their reflections on how the phenomenon of secrecy had affected their lives.

While most of the stories that are incorporated in the chapters that follow reflect emotional pain and turmoil, it is important to note that I was consistently impressed by the variety of situations that people associate with secrecy. A middle-aged newspaper editor listened to me talk about my book at a dinner party and a few days later he sent me a note: "My secret, Harriet, was that on my first communion—a very big deal in 1945 Catholic families—I was unable to swallow the wafer. It stuck to the roof of my mouth. Finally, outside after Mass, I fished it out, still dry and unswallowable, and tossed it in the grass near the church steps, sure I hadn't really become a true Catholic and surer yet that I wouldn't tell anyone . . . until you."

From a young man in his twenties, part of a sprawling Italian clan, I learned that the secret in his family is that his grandmother smokes. When grandma visits her sons and daughters and her grandchildren, she lights up in the bathroom. When she finishes, she saturates the room with Lysol to hide her crime. She's been doing it for thirty or forty years and of course everyone knows, but they would never tell her that. Grandma doesn't want to be a bad example and as far as she's concerned her two dozen plus grandchildren and great-grandkids still don't know she's a cigarette smoker.

Many of the stories that follow have qualities reminiscent of grade B soap operas. That doesn't mean they are any less touching or significant. What it means, I think, is that families are seldom ideal, that they are seldom as orderly and coherent and predictable as many of us would like to think. Families have their idiosyncrasies. Families with secrets are not unusual. Stroll around your neighborhood and think about the people who make their homes behind those doors. No doubt there are some secrets lurking there—sad ones, funny ones, just plain bizarre ones.

Sometimes I've cried while listening to the unfolding story of a family secret: how could anyone do those horrendous things to a child? Often I've gotten angry and frustrated: how could parents be so oblivious to their children's feelings? Yet there have been times too when I've laughed: whatever provoked them to make a secret out of that? The people who so generously shared their stories with me also often shared a wide range of reactions as they listened to themselves relate their experiences. I am grateful to all of them for their courage and generosity, for sharing their stories.

Introduction:
Secrets Come in Many Guises

S SSHHH. Don't tell!" As children we quickly learn the power of secrets. They ward off trouble when we've done something wrong and they give us a sense of power and control. At the same time, they separate those of us who know from those who don't.

As we grow to be adults, our secrets grow more serious, and while they continue to give us a measure of control, they also build walls between us and those we care about.

Whether our secrets are fragments of our distant past or products of our more current history, we squirrel them away in our own mental closets. But we don't forget them and often they don't forget us. Instead, secrets seem to have lives of their own, conspiring to prod us with pangs of guilt or fear, waves of sadness or shame. They crop up unexpectedly, particularly when they become germane to what's going on in our lives or the lives of those we love.

My mother told me her secret as we ambled down a dirt road in a state park, the trees resplendent, stroked in an autumn palette of red and bronze. I was in my late twenties, married, with two small boys. She was in her midsixties, a widow and a grandmother five times over.

"I was married another time," she announced out of nowhere. "Between Nat and Daddy."

"What?" I asked.

"I was married a third time," she persisted. "I had another husband."

"You did? But you never mentioned him."

"There wasn't any reason to. Until now."

I thought I understood what she meant about now. My brother Andy, three years older than me, was on the verge of a second, difficult divorce. That was why we'd all converged in central Massachusetts on this day, my mother from New York, my brother from New Hampshire, my family from Cape Ann. We'd assembled so that my brother could tell my mother in person, not on the telephone, that he and his second wife were calling it quits. I was there with my kids as a buffer.

Andy and my mother had wandered off together during the morning and apparently he had broken his news. Now she wanted to talk it out with me. I had expected that. What I hadn't expected was a third husband.

"After I got divorced from Nat, I went to Europe with John," she continued. John was my half brother, fifteen years my senior. "I married an Austrian. It was ugly. It didn't last long."

"Why are you telling me?" I asked. I was cautious, curious.

"Because I just mentioned it to Andy," she said. Defeated and lacking confidence in his ability to sustain a relationship, my brother had told my mother that he believed that maybe some people just weren't meant to be married, that maybe he was one of them. Eager to ease his pain and interject a note of optimism, she unmasked a part of her past.

"I wanted him to know that I had two failures before I met Daddy," she said. She smiled at the memory of her final marriage, a great romance that ended only with my father's death.

My image of my mother sharpened that day. The familiar qualities, her bold sense of adventure and her ability to turn strangers into soulmates in record time, were confirmed.

Barely twenty-two when John was born, she had been married several years when she divorced his father. She took off for the other side of the Atlantic with her young son in tow, back in the 1930s when women with small children did not often traipse about the world on their own.

I had known that she had spent a few years in Austria before the outbreak of World War II. She made great Wiener schnitzel and pungent goulash, skills she had learned in a Viennese cooking school. What I did not know was that her sojourn in Austria had included a miserable marriage lasting only months. I found out that much walking through the park, and nothing more.

In the years that followed, the only other information I learned from my mother was that the man's name was Hans and that he was a mountaineer. An arrogant, domineering figure, he had insisted on climbing in the Alps one day when the weather was threatening and climbers were advised to delay their expeditions. My mother tired of sitting in the lodge and went shopping. When the snow started to fall hard and the wind began to roar, whipping the landscape into a froth, Hans and his party made a premature descent. He arrived back at the lodge only to find my mother gone.

"He screamed at me," she recalled. "He said, 'How could you have left when my life was in danger?' I said, 'How could you be such an idiot as to climb under those conditions?' And that was the end of that. I was tired of sitting around and admiring him for risking his neck."

During the ensuing years I often made gentle fun of my mother. I'd say things like, "How *many* other husbands did you have?" She would laugh and say, "I can't count them all." Once, when my husband and I planned a trip to Austria, she gave us a list of names to look up. At the last minute, she crossed one off. "Annie knows everything," she murmured, "but she's probably dead by now anyway." When I pressed her, she described Annie as a distant relative of my father's, much older than he would have been, and a special friend. I never did look for her.

As the years passed, I can only remember talking about my mother's secret marriage two other times. Once I asked her, "Why didn't you ever mention Hans when we were growing up?"

"Daddy didn't want me to," she answered. "He didn't think it was anything you needed to know."

She paused thoughtfully. Then she added, "Anyway, he wanted it forgotten."

I cannot recall anything else that she said at that point but I do remember leaving the conversation with the impression that from my mother's perspective, my father had been ashamed of this chapter in her life. I wondered what cost she had paid in accepting that disapproval, and accept it she had. So effectively had she sequestered the memory of this marriage that we never guessed at its existence.

Another time I asked my mother, "How come John never mentioned anything about this stepfather, Hans?"

"I don't know," she answered. "Maybe he just wanted to forget him as much as I did." It was then that I began to recognize the extent of the pain she experienced through this union, which to me seemed so exotic. As I grew older, her secret began to reveal facets of her personality that I had never recognized.

It was not until 1988 when my mother died that I learned more. At her burial, her oldest friend told me a little about Hans. She knew his last name. She intimated that the two had become "romantically involved" while my mother was still married to John's father. My mother had gone to Nevada for a quick divorce. (An aunt later told me she thought the divorce took place in Mexico, but perhaps that was the second one.) Then my mother took off for Europe to meet her lover.

My brother John, who lives in Israel and whom I seldom see, made the trip to the States when my mother died. I asked him if he had been sworn to secrecy; why had he never mentioned horrible Hans? He had been four or five, maybe even six at the time. Didn't he remember him? John said no one had ever told him not to mention Hans. It was just a particularly miserable chapter in an already turbulent childhood, and he guessed he just never had any desire to pull the scab from the wound.

As an oil painting becomes richer with the application of each new layer of pigment, my mother's personality acquired new contours, shadows, and depths with each new revelation. She had not perhaps been such a good mother in her younger years. Just look at the facts. Ignoring the needs of a young son who had just suffered the trauma of a divorce, she carted him off to Europe, disrupting the stability of his remaining family, taking him away from his father and from grandparents who were dear to him. Then she brashly remarried, to a man who was angry, self-centered, and arrogant, in a country where my brother could not understand the language. This man too proved the wrong choice, exposing my brother to more changes and upheaval as she moved on with her life.

After separating from Hans, my mother continued to live in Europe. When war threatened, my grandparents pressured her, a Jew, to return home to the States. She refused. I learned this from an elderly aunt at my mother's memorial service. My aunt's husband, my mother's brother, took off for Europe to fetch her back. He succeeded, and on the boat during the crossing home, she met my father. The rest, as they say, is history.

I did not love my mother any less as I learned more about her. If anything, I loved her more. The knowledge of her frailties and questionable judgment humanized her for me. I was less intimidated by her intelligence, her linguistic talents, her knowledge of music, literature, history, and the arts. I had long fretted that I could not be her equal. Her secret opened up a hidden canyon filled with difficult feelings of failure, loss, impetuousness, even selfishness. All these were qualities I knew in myself. Knowing them in her made her more dear to me, less distant.

Thinking back fifteen years to the day I first learned of her hidden marriage, I recall my reactions. Who was this other husband? What was he like? Why had John never mentioned him? And most of all, what *else* didn't I know?

If a third husband could materialize from the fabric of my mother's history, what other secrets remained hidden, woven deftly into the tapestry of her life?

Beyond that, why did I suddenly have a need to know? The marriage in itself did not dismay me. The fact that it had been concealed (or perhaps more accurately, that it had never been revealed) is what troubled and intrigued me more. Did my mother distrust me? Was there something about me that made me unworthy of knowing? Did she think my respect and affection for her would be diminished if I knew of her mistake? On the other hand, was it my place to know? Was she keeping a secret from me or simply honoring her own right to privacy?

As I thought more about the way I had grown up, I realized that there was another important piece of information that had not been shared with me. It centered on my father's illness and subsequent death when I was fourteen.

Sometimes, I began to realize, a secret is not so much fact as circumstance. Sometimes it develops around the way information is handled. I knew, as my brothers knew, that my father had suffered a heart attack seven years earlier. Indeed, I had been with him when it happened.

I was eight years old and we were at the beach together, just the two of us. I wanted to swim out to a raft, farther than I had ever swum before. My father was reluctant but I pestered him and finally he agreed to go with me. When we returned to the shore, he lay face down in a few inches of water. "What are you trying to do," I asked him, "see how long you can hold your breath?" He didn't answer.

A stranger ran down to the shore, pulled my father from the water, and pounded on him. An ambulance took him away and the stranger took me home. Two weeks later my father returned from the hospital.

My impression of what that incident implied, however, was very different from that of my siblings and my mother. As far as I was concerned, my father had a heart attack, he went to the hospital, he recuperated, and he was all better. It was a scary, unhappy event, but it was over and done.

For them, there was no over and done. They knew, as I learned after his death, that his heart was scarred by the episode and damaged, and that he would never fully recover. They knew that he could die anytime. When he did die, seven years later, they grieved and I denied—for years and years and years.

The day after my father died, late at night when the visitors had gone and the house was finally quiet, I climbed up on top of a sideboard over which his portrait hung. I kissed his painted face and started talking to him and then scuttled to the floor in fright and shame as I heard my oldest brother's voice calling to me. Later that evening, I remember overhearing my mother telling my brother, "Harriet's having a hard time accepting this because she didn't expect it. She's too young to realize how weak he was, that it could have happened anytime."

For the seven years between the first and the fatal attack, my parents pretended, at least to me, that there was nothing seriously wrong. No one ever talked to me about my father's illness. No one talked to me about what happened at the beach (would he have been alright if I hadn't made him swim so far?) and what that meant in terms of the future. I don't remember visiting him in the hospital either.

They kept his illness from me in order to spare me from uncertainty and sadness. The problem is, I always knew that there was something wrong but I also knew that I wasn't supposed to talk about it. And when my father died, I refused to talk about that.

I didn't go to his funeral. I kept up, for years, the fantasy that my father was away on a long business trip. And it took me years to figure out that I was furious, not at my father for dying, but at both my parents for keeping his illness from me. I was furious because in their eyes, I reasoned, I had been too immature, too little to be part of something so important to my family.

When I talked about my sense of exclusion with my oldest brother many years later, he was defensive. "It wasn't that anyone kept anything from you deliberately," he said. And I believe he was mostly right.

What my family did was to make a collective yet unconscious choice to protect me, the youngest, by shielding me from the pain that would have gone with acknowledging that my father was, in a sense, living on borrowed time. But another way to look at the same scenario is to say that by taking this tack they isolated me. By shielding me, they left me feeling that I was too insignificant to be part of what was happening. By choosing to shelter me from the truth, they deprived me of the opportunity to become accustomed to the reality of my father's waning health and to come to grips with my feelings of fear and sadness.

Because I did not share the knowledge of his illness, it was difficult for me to be able to mourn for him when he died. And although my mother and my brothers and close friends and relatives did their best to include me in their embrace, it was difficult for me to share the comfort and support they extended to each other following his death because I had not been a full participant in the experience that led our family to that moment. The secret of my father's illness was more amorphous than the secret of my mother's third marriage, yet it had formidable consequences in terms of my own development.

Thinking hard about what it means to share and to withhold information, I began to realize that there is still another kind of secret that frequently forms in a family, and that is the secret that centers on disguising or concealing the way a member of a family is feeling. I recall learning from my mother, when I was an adult with a family of my own, that all the years I had thought one of my brothers had a standing weekly appointment with a special dentist he was actually seeing a psychiatrist.

She told me too of a favorite cousin who had had a baby in a far corner of the world and given her up for adoption. And she confided that she and my father had stopped seeing their closest friends, people I had grown up feeling related to, because the man had tried to initiate an affair with my mother. As I think about these disclosures, I do not experience the sense of imbalance and the need to know that I felt when I learned of my mother's third marriage, or the anger and feelings of exclusion I experienced when I realized everyone else in my family knew how sick my father was, when I watched them grieve for him while I was unable to admit that he was dead. I began to wonder about the line between secrecy and privacy and how it ought to be drawn. Whose secret is it anyway?

Most of us associate the intentional manipulative use of secrecy with corporations and governments. Businesses resort to secrecy as a means of protecting their research efforts or the possible replication of their existing products or procedures. We know that security clearances are required to work in certain industries, particularly with respect to government contracts, and we are familiar with agencies like the Secret Service and the CIA. We recognize that secrecy is employed to disguise illegal and immoral acts as well as to protect legitimate interests.

Yet secrecy is also a mechanism or strategy to which many of us turn, to a greater or lesser degree, in our daily interactions with friends and families, lovers and neighbors, and other individuals whose paths cross ours. Family secrets are often kept around issues of pregnancy, birth, miscarriage, abortion, adoption, marriage, divorce, death, physical and mental illness, and alcohol and drug dependencies.

Secrecy is one tool we use to adapt to what has happened to us. Through the conscious, deliberate concealment or disclosure of information, we take some control of our lives and exercise a degree of power over those with whom we interact. As with corporations and governments, the more information others have about us, the more predictable our behavior becomes to them.

Secrecy provides a layer of protection. The less vulnerable we are, the less we open ourselves to the possibility of reaction and encroachment. On the other hand, secrecy can prevent us from seeking support and, eventually, peace of mind. In concealing our errors and shortcomings, we deprive ourselves of the opportunity to be forgiven, understood, comforted, and accepted as we are.

While some secrets are conscious, purposeful efforts designed to hide information, others are formed inadvertently or unconsciously. They develop because they involve painful feelings that we are unable to confront. At times, secrets develop simply because no one figures out that an event took place. It is not that the event has been concealed, but rather that it has gone undiscovered.

When I was eighteen I became pregnant. I married shortly after and gave birth to a son. Two more children followed in later years. One day when my oldest son was in the fifth grade he was assigned a social studies project that required him to research his family tree. He asked me some questions including the date of my marriage. Suddenly he turned to me and said with considerable agitation, "So how pregnant were you anyway when you got married?"

I answered, "about two months," and his anger faded as quickly as it had grown. Why? I think because I gave him the information he wanted matter-of-factly, calmly. Had I answered defensively or had I started to fudge on the dates to cover up my "mistake," I think I would have both undermined his trust in me and given him a sense of shame concerning his own beginnings. I had not purposefully concealed from him the fact that I was pregnant with him when I got married, that I "had" to get married, as he put it. I had simply never found an appropriate time or way to pass the information on to him. I had never lied about the number of years I'd been married or the date of my anniversary. And when my son was old enough to put the pieces together, he made the discovery himself. I do not know if or when I would have told him had he not asked. It just didn't seem very important to me. And yet I must admit to a sense of relief once we shared ownership of the information.

Often people keep secrets because they fear the shame they expect to experience should others, particularly those they love, become party to their less than respectable behavior or personal qualities. A woman goes to great lengths to conceal an abortion. A man rewrites his military experience to disguise the fact that he was discharged from the service because he had a nervous breakdown during boot camp. In still other instances secrets are kept to spare the feelings of others in the family, as when a Baptist woman leaves home and marries a Jewish man and hides her husband's religious background from her devout parents. One has to ask, however, whether her motivation is actually to spare her parents or to spare herself the anguish of coming clean with them.

Frequently secrets form to protect a person's public persona. While an actor might find it unnecessary to hide his homosexuality, it may be expedient for an aspiring lawyer to conceal exactly the same information. Similarly, politicians and other public figures might resort to secrecy when faced with problems requiring psychiatric help because they fear the consequences the disclosure would have on their careers.

In many instances secrecy is oriented toward a goal as when people keep secrets for practical reasons. An illegal Mexican immigrant hides his status in order to avoid deportation. An adolescent hides copies of *Playboy* beneath his mattress to avoid punishment or ridicule from his parents. A boy signs up for ballet lessons—in a neighboring town—because he fears embarrassment should his friends discover he likes to dance.

As parents, we usually keep secrets from our children because we want to protect both them and ourselves. We are afraid that our children will greet our revelations with tears, with fury, with angry recriminations. In short, we are afraid of the emotional upheaval and pain we will unleash in both ourselves and in our kids. We're afraid too that they will see us as dishonest, undermining their sense of trust in us. All of these consequences are indeed possible.

Uncorking a secret can evoke hurt and fear and shame. But it can also enrich our lives and those of our children by allowing us to know each other clear through to the bone, providing a matrix in which we can struggle to accept each other as we genuinely are, complete with lumps and warts.

The more I thought about concealed information and the way it affects families, the more I realized that I needed to explore the phenomena of secrets in families other than my own. It is my purpose then to collect, relate, and interpret the stories of others who have kept family secrets or who have uncovered them. I want to discover their motivations for both withholding and disclosing information. I want to explore how the transmittal of the information affects the ways members of a family perceive and treat each other and themselves.

Keeping a secret implies exclusion. There are those who know and those who don't. If knowledge is indeed power, what does the use of secrecy say about the way power is distributed in a family? How do secrets evolve? Is there manipulation involved? What happens when a secret is broken inadvertently? Is there a healthy, appropriate use of secrecy? How does secrecy affect the interplay between different generations within a family? How does our culture reinforce the use of secrecy? These are some of the questions I explore in *Family Secrets*.

1

Where Did I Come From?

T HE meaning of a question varies according to who is doing the asking and why. We know that children are able to absorb and internalize increasingly complex information as they grow older. Their capacities to reason and to understand become increasingly sophisticated and their need to know demands more detailed responses as their sphere of experience broadens. While the words spoken may be identical, the question asked by a four year old and a fourteen year old may be an entirely different one. In order to respond to the query satisfactorily, we need to be able to decipher the hidden concerns that hide behind the words and to accurately identify the type of information the interrogator seeks. At times, the question is not even asked. It is instead wondered about, mulled over, disguised perhaps by a less threatening request.

As parents, we have an almost automatic reflex to the question, "Where did I come from?" That's the birds and the bees question, we tell ourselves. Time to launch into an explanation of the union of the sperm and the egg and the subsequent beginnings of a new life. Although our own background, attitude toward sex, values, and inhibitions color the information we impart and the way we do it, we know that there is a factually correct answer to the question. It is a matter of getting the biology straight and conveying it to the child clearly.

But sometimes the need to know has overtones. Often kids ask follow-up questions such as "How does the sperm get to the egg?" Do they ever ask, "Whose sperm was it anyway?" They may not ask aloud. They may not recognize the existence of the question in their own minds. They may not even think to wonder, and yet for some people, the matter of parentage eventually emerges as a powerful family issue, an issue that often becomes couched in shame, lies, and confusion.

Social scientists have argued the nature-versus-nurture question for decades. They debate the extent to which an individual's personality is biologically determined by the genetic matter built into our chromosomes versus the way in which we were raised. The issue of parentage illustrates the ambiguity, inconsistencies, and inadequacies that emerge when the source of the biological contribution is clouded. What happens when a man learns that the person he thought was his father really isn't his father? What does it feel like to discover that your brother or sister has a different father from you? How might a teenager feel when he inadvertently discovers that he was adopted? What kinds of secrets develop around parentage and whom do they affect?

Alicia

When Alicia Lord was eighteen, she had an illegal abortion. Her parents knew about it, indeed they helped finance it. Several months later, she married the man who fathered the aborted child. She knew the union was a mistake right from the start, but she felt that the marriage would make her respectable. Marrying John would show that she was not just a promiscuous kid, sleeping around. She felt that getting married would legitimize what had happened.

A year later, she found herself pregnant again. The marriage was faring poorly but, she says, "Having gone through an abortion, there was no way I was going to go through another. Anyway, I wanted this baby very badly."

She developed severe back problems early in the pregnancy and, at her doctor's urging, quit her job. She spent that summer with her parents at their summer beach house on Long Island, while John stayed in New Haven to continue with his graduate studies, visiting her on weekends. When they were together, they socialized frequently with a friend named Wally, who was staying with his parents in the same summer community. Soon Alicia and Wally began to spend increasing amounts of time together during the week. It wasn't long before she became deeply involved with him, and although she initially tried to resist the relationship, she soon realized that she was a lot happier with Wally than with John. Alicia decided that she was going to leave her husband, regardless of how things worked out with Wally. At the end of August, she returned to New Haven, told John she wanted to be with Wally, and packed up. She returned to New Haven once more in September, and that's the last time she ever saw John.

"Wally knew from the moment we met at the beach that I was pregnant," she recalls, "and he never thought there was anything wrong with that." They began to live together when she was about ten weeks along, so, she explains, "we really went through the whole pregnancy together." They planned to marry as soon as they could and Wally was delighted about the prospect of parenthood from the start. "I think I never quite believed him when he said it made absolutely no difference to him that he wasn't the biological father, but he's never wavered," she observes.

John fainted when Alicia told him she was leaving. Yet despite the intensity of this initial reaction, he never pursued her or his child. He came from a wealthy family and his grandfather had died recently, leaving John as one of his heirs. When it became clear that a divorce was imminent, the family lawyer was very eager for John to relinquish his paternal rights because he feared that Alicia would try to lay claim to some of his inheritance in the child's interest. Consequently, John went to Mexico to file for divorce (Alicia was too pregnant to travel).

She was living with Wally but still legally married to John when the baby was born. "We did the whole thing straight," she recalls. "I went into the hospital under my currently married name and I put John's name down on the birth certificate, but Wally was with me in labor."

Wally's father and brother came to visit at the hospital. His mother had passed away two months earlier, Alicia recalls. "She had decided that Wally was really the father, that he and I had been screwing around. That's how she handled it. Well, she was dying and if she needed that, that was alright. I told her, 'If that's what you want to believe, then you go ahead and believe that.'"

Wally and Alicia returned home from the hospital with their new son, Max, and Wally quickly went through the steps of legal adoption. "Wally has never, to this day," explains Alicia, "acted in any way other than that this is his child. No less, no more, in his mind, than our daughter Sophie. I had a little bit more trouble with it, not that I ever felt he treated Max any differently. I guess it was for the same reason that I had trouble believing that my father didn't really want a son." (Alicia is the youngest of three sisters.) "I grew up in a generation where you always heard that every man wants a son. And here I was the last of my father's children, and another daughter. Somewhere deep inside of me I couldn't believe that Wally didn't really want his own child, so it was very important to me to get pregnant again. I had a miscarriage, and then when Max was almost three I had Sophie."

When she became pregnant with Sophie, Alicia began to think about how and when to tell Max that Wally was not his biological father. She was very conscientious in preparing him for a new baby, but she always found reasons to delay telling him about his own origins. It weighed less heavily on Wally, though he too was concerned. "It's not like outright adoption where you start telling the child right from the beginning so that it's knowledge he grows up with," Alicia muses. "I am, always was, and always will be Max's mother, and in every respect except one moment in time, Wally is Max's father. Of course, there are tremendous implications from that moment. But it's different from the two of us choosing to adopt a baby. And I just kept thinking this was something that a child needed to be older to understand."

In the course of grappling with how to tell Max the truth, Alicia spent an afternoon with a friend whose father had died recently. In going through family files with her mother, the daughter found divorce papers documenting a marriage her mother had made long before marrying her father. The daughter had never heard of this marriage and she felt betrayed and distrustful.

"She was emphatic in saying that I had to tell Max his story, that I owed him the truth," Alicia recalls. "It confirmed my feeling that this was something Max had a right to know. It's his story. It's his history. And I also knew as a practical matter that as he grew up his health was going to be influenced to some degree by the history of someone he'd never known."

It has been well documented that pathological behaviors such as child abuse and alcoholism run in families, that patterns are prone to repetition, sometimes skipping a generation or two and sometimes not. As much as we may deplore and ache from the pain inflicted on us as children, somewhere in our fabric we absorb the coping mechanisms of those who are dear to us. They are our models, whether we like it or not. And sometimes, despite ourselves, we find that we are following the same path. At times we are conscious of this, as when a young mother slaps her wailing infant and at the same moment relives the sting of her own mother's hand. Knowing that this is wrong does not mean she can simply stop. Sometimes the history is hidden. We didn't consciously realize that our responsible, go-to-work-every-morning father was an alcoholic, or that our parents hated each other even though they disappeared behind the same bedroom door every night.

In Alicia's story, John, Max's biological father, never made any effort to see or contact his son, who is now in his early twenties. The lack of contact gave Alicia the opportunity to avoid dealing with her dilemma. If John had been a presence, she would probably have felt compelled to offer Max an explanation. If John had chosen to be recognized as his son's father, the secret of Max's paternity would never have developed.

Looking at John's family history, his behavior toward his child appears a reflection of his heritage. His own father had married twice and John was the product of the second marriage. His father and his first wife had a baby, and when the child was about a year and a half old, the marriage fell apart. After moving out, John's father gave up all contact with his daughter. When John was about twelve, his parents took him and his younger sister out to North Dakota to meet some elderly relatives. According to Alicia, this was the first and only time John met his father's family, including his own half sister, who was married and in her twenties. This was also the only time John's father had seen his oldest daughter since she was a toddler. "His father had gotten married very young and had a baby right away," she recalls, "and he never saw her, so I think on some level John had this sense that this happens, that it's okay to walk away."

When Max was six, Alicia found herself feeling tremendously overwrought about some problems he was having in school. She can't remember what the difficulty involved, but she vividly recalls feeling responsible for his unhappiness. "I think I was just feeling very guilty, like I had deprived him on some level even though intellectually I knew full well that the parenting and love he got from Wally, and the life we had in New York, were far richer than we would have had if I had stayed with John— because I think I would have ended up getting divorced from him later anyway, but it would have been a different kind of divorce and a different situation. I think I felt that I owed Max something and I think I needed someone to give me some guidance." Although it was not clear to her then, Alicia now realizes that what she owed Max was not the perfect beginning that she could not give him, but something much more attainable—the simple truth.

She remembers having a conference with Max's teacher and ending up in tears. It was then that she told the teacher her story, Max's story, which she had shared with hardly anyone. The teacher calmly but firmly made it clear that she felt Max needed to be let in on the secret. "I think she understood," Alicia speculates, "that by not telling him, it was building up inside of me, and that my confusion was starting to get in the way of my relationship with Max. I told her that I wanted to tell him, but I never could think of a way to say it. Every time I came up with a way in my mind, it sounded very negative. And I didn't want to say John was a bad man . . . because he wasn't."

The teacher offered Alicia a simple, straightforward solution. Why did she have to assign any value judgment to the information at all? Why couldn't she just state the facts, that when she and Wally met, she was pregnant with Max? "It was a major revelation to me," Alicia says, shaking her head. "Not to go into any explanation about the marriage or about what had gone wrong. Max didn't need that. Certainly not at that age. And it lifted such an enormous burden from my shoulders that I couldn't wait to get home and tell him."

Tell him she did, together with Wally. "It was like suddenly the clouds parted and there was this brilliant sunlight," she remembers. "It was so direct, and I've never been very good at being direct. I always had to deal with the overlays before getting to the heart of the matter. It was such a relief."

Max's reaction was matter-of-fact. He had seen pictures of Alicia and Wally together with both their dogs as well as Wally's parents' dog and he asked, "Oh, was that the summer you took the pictures with Zeb and Luke and Sukey?" Alicia said yes, it was. Max didn't pursue the subject much, although she does remember talking with him about what it means to be a daddy. "I think he might have said, 'Do you mean my daddy isn't really my daddy?' and I said, 'Does being a daddy mean spending time together and doing things together and loving and helping each other?' and he said, 'Yes, of course,' and I said, 'Well, then you've got the best daddy there is.' " She thinks that what Max was really doing was seeking reassurance, that he was asking, "Am I going to be as important to him, to my daddy, as I would be if he were my biological father?"

As she looks back, she remembers thinking it odd that he didn't ask more questions—specific ones about who his natural father was, where he was, what he did—but now that he's grown and his personality has crystallized, she thinks she understands why. "He's a very internal person. He doesn't let you know how he's feeling a lot of the time and I don't think I realized that then. He was six and a half. Up to then he'd been very much a little kid. If he was angry, he'd stamp his foot. If he was happy, he'd laugh. But then he was just at the age when he was starting to venture out into the world, so his more adult personality was beginning to form."

The sense of relief that Alicia experienced once she told Max the truth is not uncommon. While part of it can be attributed to the fact that she no longer had to fret over when and how to tell him, a greater part probably can be traced back to her remark that she felt guilty and responsible for whatever difficulties beset her child at the time. Perhaps Alicia felt that no matter how successfully she had pulled her life together, no matter how good a father Wally proved to be, still, she had gotten her son off to a less than storybook start and that, therefore, she had to shoulder a disproportionate share of the pain and confusion and angst he experienced in the normal order of growing up. Once all the cards were on the table, she could relate to him clearly and directly, no longer inadvertently putting pressure on herself to atone for the past.

In the months and years that followed, Max showed little curiosity about his biological father. Alicia seldom brought up the subject but she did keep the door open by not covering up the time she spent as John's wife. She might say something like, "Well that happened when I lived in New Haven and I was pregnant with you," but she basically believed that she should take her cues from Max. Since he hardly ever asked questions, Alicia said little. She does, however, recall a time about three years later, when Max was nearly ten.

An avid baseball fan, Max had realized that there was a star player who had the same name as his biological father and he asked Alicia if the man happened to be his dad. She said no. He asked several more questions over the next day or two, and then dropped the subject completely.

Sophie, on the other hand, showed persistent interest. She was four when Alicia and Wally told Max the secret, and the few times the family did talk about it, she was present because Alicia didn't want to slide the story into a dark corner now that she'd gotten it out in the open. Alicia interprets Sophie's concern as her way of trying to sort out the differences between herself and her brother. "There's been a lot of tension between the two of them since day one," she explains. "As a little boy, Max would say that the worst day in his life was when we brought Sophie home from the hospital. They're so different from one another. I think on one level Sophie's curiosity is her way to process the differences between them, a way to explain why their personalities and styles are as different as night and day."

Both kids are sociable and outgoing, but Sophie tends to be far more expressive in terms of her feelings. "If she gets angry, she's impossible for two minutes, five minutes, an hour, and then it all blows away. If Max gets angry, he'll brood and hold things inside and you won't even know it, but it colors how he reacts to people," she observes. Sophie tends to be artistic, avant-garde, while Max is more middle of the road. As Alicia puts it, "I think she sees him as a sort of stick-in-the-mud and he sees her as doing things just for effect." She also thinks Sophie's curiosity about Max's natural father is a way for Sophie to rationalize, as she says, "that the chances of her being like him are minimal. I think in that way she sees it as a comfort."

Sophie, now a teenager, is away at boarding school and Max is a college student, yet Sophie continues to ask questions about her brother and his natural father. She wants to know if Max looks like him. She wants to know if he will ever meet him and she wants to know why he doesn't show much curiosity about him. Yet neither Max or Sophie has ever asked to see a photograph of John. When Alicia's mother died recently she found an album of wedding photos of herself and John and she took it home. "I have it," she says, "not on the coffee table, but I have it. It's a piece of my history." If her children ask, she will show it to them.

Similarly, although she would never do the legwork for Max, Alicia would have no problem offering him the little information she has about John's whereabouts, should he decide at some point that he wants to find his natural father. Yet even though she is no longer married to him, she worries about how Wally would react to such an effort. "Wally claims that it would be fine with him but I've always felt that on some level he would be hurt by this, if Max wanted to do it. But that's me, that's my fear. If he's hurt, he's hurt. He'll have to deal with it. Max has to do what he has to do, and if he decides he has to meet John, then that's what he has to do."

Toni

A journalist now in her late twenties, Toni Barkley grew up in Minnesota, the eldest daughter in the only black family in town in a state with a minority population below two percent. Toni's mother had her first child, a son, when she was just seventeen. Toni was born when she was nineteen and another daughter followed three years later. Partly because her mother was so young and partly because of the isolation she felt from her peers because of her race, Toni became extraordinarily close to her mother. The two always spent Friday nights together and, Toni explains, "I would always tell her everything in the world, every single little detail. Sometimes, as I got to be a teenager, she would say, 'Toni, you can't tell me everything. I'm your mother!' "

But Toni continued to confide, even after she headed off for college in Georgia, her first experience living away from home. There she became involved with a young man and had sex for the first time. She immediately telephoned home to let her mother know.

Toni and the boy were both involved in what she calls a "Christian quasi cult" on campus. "I was thinking," she says, " 'Oh my God, we shouldn't be doing this because we're not married.' But I was also all excited about it. So I called my mother and said, 'Look, this is what happened, but we're going to pray about it and we're not going to do it again.' One part of me was saying, 'I'm not going to do that anymore, I can't do it,' and the other part was cheering, 'I did it! I did it!' "

Toni's mother had said to her from the time she was a little girl, that if she ever wanted to be sexually active, just to let her know and together they would go and get her appropriate birth control. She had said, "It doesn't matter how old you are. It doesn't matter what I think. Just let me know and we'll get it." So as Toni shared her news and insisted that her religious convictions would prevent a repeat performance, her mother recognized the schism and addressed it. "She said, 'Toni, you're going to be going from the bed to your knees, from your knees to the bed, from the bed to your knees.' Then she added, 'Just like your grandmother said, sex is like a narcotic. Once you start you're not going to stop.' "

Toni continued to argue that she wasn't going to do it anymore and her mother kept trying to get her to be realistic. "I just wasn't facing up to it as an adult," Toni remarks now, "and I think that's what she was seeing. I wasn't being rational. Finally, to shake me up a bit and say 'Hey, this is real life and you need to deal with it,' she said to me, 'Look, the first time I had sex, I got pregnant.' " Toni had never, as she puts it, "done the numbers," so she asked, "Is that when you and daddy decided to get married?"

"No," her mother answered. "You and your brother don't have the same father."

The revelation stopped Toni cold. When she thinks back on it, she remembers feeling terribly betrayed. There was nothing she would not tell her best friend, her mother, and yet her mother had kept this enormous truth from her.

"I was seventeen," she says, "and I was sure she had been as candid with me as I had been with her. I felt angry, but I don't know what I was angry at, whether it was at her or whether it was the fact that Frank wasn't really my brother. All of a sudden I was losing my friend and my brother too. I was really angry."

She remembers too a gush of questions. Does my brother know that? Where's his father? Who is he? What happened to him? Does everyone else in the family know? Her mother didn't tell her who the father was but she did tell her very calmly that Toni's own father formally adopted Frank when he was three. She told her that her brother had been told the secret when he was around thirteen. She told her too that her aunts knew, her grandmother knew, and her great-grandmother as well. After they hung up the phone, they only talked about it one more time, and that was several years later.

Toni told the secret to her roommate, who in turn told her a secret about her family involving a pregnancy out of wedlock. "Next thing you know," Toni says, "we were talking to someone else who had a secret and we started thinking, God, black families have all these skeletons in their closets." But her worries began to abate as she talked to more and more of the girls in her dormitory and "discovered that nearly everyone had something like this." The frequency made her feel better. "I thought, 'my family isn't all screwed up. Everybody's got their quirks.'"

As she looks back on her experience, Toni believes the truth about her brother's paternity explains a lot of unanswered questions and clarifies certain incidents that happened in her family. Her brother, for example, is very tall, while she and her sister and mother are all around 5′5″ and her father is a bit shorter than that.

"I'd always wondered," she says, "where we got this big boy, 6′4″, two hundred and some pounds. And he's huge: big arms, big legs. My father's a teeny-weeny man." Also, she says, her brother's hair is very straight and smooth while the rest of the family has coarse hair. When she and her sister played with him as children, they teased him, saying, "You don't look like us."

"My father always seemed to be a little bit angry about my brother's height," she says, recalling a day when the whole family loaded into the car and her brother got in back and asked his father if he could move up the front seat a little. "My father blew up," she says. "He screamed something like, 'If your legs are too long, just cut them off.' "

Toni's father is a research biologist and she remembers another incident when she was a high school student. Her biology class was studying dominant and recessive genes and Toni decided to try to figure out why her brother was so tall while the rest of the family was short. She knew her mother's father was pretty tall and she speculated that maybe her father's father was taller too. "I made a chart to explain how it all could have happpened," she says, and "I ran home and said, 'Daddy, I figured out why Frank's so tall.' " She was very excited, expecting her father to be proud of her efforts. "We were standing in the kitchen and I remember seeing that my mother looked apprehensive. I was explaining all this and saying, 'I've solved the riddle!' and my father said, 'Families don't talk about these kinds of things' and stomped off. And I thought there's his anger again. But I didn't know what it was all about."

Several years after learning the secret, Toni decided to pass the story on to her younger sister. She did it, she thinks, not so much out of an obligation to share the truth with her sister but because "I guess I just had to tell someone else who was close to it. Maybe I wanted someone else to be as surprised as I was."

Toni realizes now that secrecy is nothing new in her family. "My mother was a secret herself in a way, and one secret begets another," she explains. When Toni's grandmother was sixteen, she got involved with a married man who left her alone and pregnant in Minnesota. The grandmother didn't want anyone to know of her condition, so she took off for Georgia where she stayed with an aunt until the baby, Toni's mother, was born. Eventually the grandmother's own mother fetched her and the infant back to Minnesota, where Toni's mother grew up. At sixteen she made a trip to Louisiana to visit her father. At seventeen she had a baby, whom she named Frank. Her father's middle name is also Frank.

"My sister and I had this odd notion that his father might be our grandfather. It just makes sense. We found ourselves putting together dates and places and then it was like, let's just leave this alone and not think about it anymore. It's such a strong possibility that neither of us wanted to look at it any closer."

Toni remembers asking her mother if Frank wanted to find his natural father. She remembers her mother saying that if she wanted to know that, she should ask Frank. That Toni has never broached the subject with him she attributes to the differences in their personalities and political views, which she describes as absolute opposites. He is conservative, she is liberal. He is a career officer in the Armed

Services. She is an investigative reporter. But she also suspects he wouldn't want to deal with it.

"He's not very good at sorting out emotional issues or even acknowledging them," Toni says. "He'd say, 'This is too painful for me to talk about,' and what he'd really mean is 'I don't want to find out who my father is because then I'd want to know why he left and no excuse would be good enough for me.' "

It is clear, however, that Toni is torn between imposing her own values on Frank and leaving him alone to make sense of his origins as he sees fit, in the privacy of his own thoughts and feelings.

"If it were me," she says, "I would want to know. So I would assume he would want to know. Of course, he's not me and maybe he really doesn't want to."

Toni speculates that the secret probably evolved because Frank's conception and birth were rooted in a time that was very unhappy for their mother. Secrecy is often used as a tool for forgetting the past.

"As a family we don't talk about the sad times," Toni says. "Our memories are built on accomplishments. Sort of an attitude that bad things belong in the past and let's just keep on living and looking forward."

As she thinks through her own experience in learning of her brother's paternity and adoption, Toni says, "I had thought of Frank as my full brother for seventeen years, so to hear about it at that age doesn't change a thing between us. For a second it did. I felt lost, like my brother was taken away, but just for a moment."

Her relationship with her mother, however, did change. Looking back, Toni senses that the change was necessary and inevitable. Although provoked by the revelation of the secret, it was a change which needed to happen anyway. "We had been so close," she says, "that we needed to separate for awhile so that we could come back together and know each other as adults. But at the time, I felt just like you feel about a friend who withholds information. Just kind of cold. I'd always trusted my mother. Why didn't she trust me? So I started telling her less. I started sharing more with the girls in the dormitory. I think that's when we started going from being close friends to being more mother and daughter."

Martin

Martin Dare found out about his past quite innocently, in a conversation with his girlfriend when he was sixteen.

"I don't know exactly what we were talking about," he recalls, struggling to recreate the moment of disclosure twenty-seven years later, "but she said something like, 'Well, I can understand why you'd think that, being adopted.' I said, 'What?' And then I kind of froze."

Reflecting back, he realizes that living in a small, island community, it was almost inevitable that he would find out one day. His girlfriend's parents knew his parents and some of the Dare family history. They had talked about it with their daughter, who never realized that she knew more than Martin did about his own origins.

Martin didn't doubt his girlfriend's announcement. In a way, it made sense. "Both my parents are naturally blonde and I've got curly black hair," he says. The revelation solved other small puzzles too, like why there weren't any photographs of him until he was about two. And he'd always wondered why his birth certificate showed he was born in Boston when in the 1940s it was almost unheard of for a woman from his Maine village to make the long trek south just to have a baby. But at the same time that it answered questions, knowledge of his adoption scrambled up his basic assumptions about his place in the world. "Instead of having a clearly delineated history," he explains, "parents, grandparents, national origin—it was like starting with a blank." He felt let down. Most of all, it confirmed his sense that throughout his childhood, his parents had been less than upfront with him on lots of issues.

"I was brought up in an environment," he remembers, "where lots of things weren't talked about. Unpleasant things. Both of my parents were married before, but that was never discussed and I learned it somewhere else, not from them." Sex too was shrouded in secrecy. In fact, the only time he can remember his father bringing up the subject was once when he had had too much to drink. And although the family lived comfortably, his father was very secretive about their financial picture. "My father had loads of money," he says, "but he spent it inconspicuously. I think he felt people would take advantage of him, and that's something that rubbed off on me. Because of my financial condition, after inheriting from him, I started to react the way he did, in terms of being secretive and suspicious."

Martin's mother was a housewife and his father spent most of the time at work or socializing. He was, Martin says, "consumed with making money." The household was oriented toward adults and Martin learned early on that the way to win his parents' approval was to be retiring and compliant. "Our house was like a cocktail party," he says. "My father would bring businesss people home almost every day after work and they'd stay until all hours. And my father was very smart. We had one of the first TVs on the block, a huge box with a tiny picture, and he concocted this device where I could sit in front of the set with earphones on and he could switch the sound off. Basically, I could be invisible." Since having a child seemed out of sync with the way his parents lived their lives, Martin finds it difficult to imagine why they adopted him. Maybe, he says, it was because their friends had children. Maybe it was to have someone to carry on the family name.

Martin reacted to the revelation of his adoption by stuffing it away. It was after all a family secret. He wasn't supposed to know about it. In fact, he became a partner in the conspiracy—he has never told his parents that he knows.

Martin's father died when he was twenty, but his mother is still alive today, yet he still has not broached the subject. It is clear, though, that Martin has never truly set it aside.

"I'm curious," he says, "but I also have fear of addressing it. I want to know what there is to know. But on the other side of the coin, I don't really want to know. Because there are real parents who gave me up, which is about the ultimate rejection. Sometimes I think that maybe I should talk to my mother about it. Actually, it's more of an issue for my wife than for me. She thinks it would be healthy but I'm not so sure. I don't see what's to be gained at this point."

He admits that there have been opportunities to raise the subject but, he says quietly, "I haven't chosen to, dared to, or whatever." Partly, he is afraid of hurting her feelings. She is the only mother he has known and he doesn't want her to think that he's unhappy about their relationship.

And he is a little worried that she might react by saying simply, "Oh gee, I thought you were well aware of that," minimizing the importance all over again.

When asked if he feels he has a secret from his mother, withholding from her the fact that he knows he's adopted, Martin says, "That's true. I guess it's a tradition."

Another part of that tradition, he says, is a fundamental lack of openness in relationships. He wishes that he had been told he was adopted for the same reason that he wishes there had been more genuine openness and honesty in his family.

"It hurt to find out from a source outside the immediate family," he says, "which wouldn't have happened if I had been told from the start. And it hurts that there wasn't much emotional openness."

Being emotionally closed is a trait that he works to overcome and a pattern he tries to break by consciously keeping his own children in touch with the truth about their family. He has told his two daughters, who are twelve and three, that he is adopted. And although he will not tell his mother that he knows of his adoption, he has also not told his girls to avoid the subject with their grandmother because, he says, "I don't believe in having kids lie or cover up. They know what they know. Honesty's important."

It is as though he is determined that his own children will not suffer the same absurdity he has experienced, namely, "Do I know what I know or don't I know it?" In adulthood, Martin has not yet fully come to terms with that question with his mother. With his wife and his children, however, he thinks that he is making progress. If he hadn't, he says, his family might have been destroyed when his business recently came upon hard times.

"Our finances have changed dramatically for the worse," he confides, "but I think my attitude has changed dramatically for the better. If it hadn't changed, in the direction of being more emotionally open, I think we probably would have divorced. If you have a real partnership, I think sharing is very important, whether it's good news or bad news."

Martin concludes, "I don't think it's ever too late to change. Here I am listening to myself say all this and now I'm thinking maybe I should deal with it with my mother. Maybe having it out in the open would be a burden off of her as well as me. . . ."

The more directly the secret bears upon the individual's life, the wiser it appears to be to dissipate it as early as possible. The more it affects that person, the more he or she deserves to share ownership of the information.

2

My Father's Other Child

A S children, the amount we know about our parents'
history is largely dependent upon their willingness to
share their past with us. In many families, fathers and
mothers read their children a tightly edited version of their
life story. They highlight the experiences that they value
and minimize, color, or altogether eliminate those that
have left them with twinges of shame or disappointment.
For many of us, the image we hold of our parents' lives is
a collage assembled from scant pieces of solid information
embellished with the fruit of our own imagination, the
speculations that those fragments evoke in us. We may
have heard whispers of a tumultuous youth, we may have
stumbled on puzzling contradictions or gaps in our parents' rendition of their histories, we may be party to an
accepted set of family stories which give us a glimpse of
their past, but for the most part we tend not to pry.

As children, what is important in our lives is the present.
In our relationship with our parents, what matters most to

us as we grow up is their actions and emotions at the moment, as they directly relate to us. As we emerge into adulthood, a shift occurs. No longer as self-absorbed as when we were younger, we begin to wonder about the shadows we've sensed, the inconsistencies we've accepted as just part of the way things are. We begin to put pieces together, to discern patterns. More than that, we begin to talk to our parents adult to adult, and in doing so we sometimes discover more than we bargained for. We are forced to acknowledge that our parents were not always parents, that they had their own lives well before they had us, that they had passions and crises of their own. Sometimes they had lovers. Sometimes they had other children, children we didn't know about.

To discover a sibling that we never knew of is to discover a part of ourselves. As with most discoveries relating to our own identity, finding a half brother or sister can activate a chain of emotions ranging from anger to confusion, feelings of betrayal, sadness, uncertainty, and sometimes joy. The existence of a half brother or sister does not in itself appear to rock our sense of self. It is instead the uncertainties about those who kept the information from us that we tend to find unsettling. If our parent could conceal such a vital part of himself or herself from us, we wonder, how well do we really know that parent?

Joel

Following a successful career in law enforcement, including a stint as a top-notch detective for a major metropolitan police department, Joel Abramson turned entrepreneur. Today he oversees a flourishing fish importing business and lives amid the trappings of success. Sitting with him in the sunroom of the luxurious house where he and his wife and three teenage children live, it is difficult to imagine him in a lesser situation, but when he tells about the part secrecy played in his family, the story evokes a far humbler setting.

Joel grew up in a two-bedroom apartment in Brooklyn, where his father ran a fish market. He had a brother six years older than he, and a sister sixteen years older who married and moved out when he was just three.

His mother came from Russia and his father from Poland and as he thinks back, he realizes he knows nothing of their childhoods, nothing prior to their having met in this country when they were already adults. He got his first taste of a family secret when he was nine.

One night while his parents were out and his brother was babysitting, Joel got it into his head to check out the tin box stored in the top of the linen closet. He had been told that the box held all the family records and pictures but he had never looked inside it.

"That particular night," he reminisces, "I climbed way to the top of the closet. Of course it was just the top shelf, but when I was nine years old it seemed a long way up. I remember having to put something on top of a chair to give me the height. I really made an effort." He reached for the box and brought it down. He found some wedding pictures stuffed among the papers, and when he looked closely, it dawned on him that the woman in the photos wasn't his mother. There was also a marriage certificate that wasn't in his mother's name.

Curious and forthright, he woke his father early the next morning to tell him about his fascinating discovery. His father explained, with his mother present, that when

Joel's sister Mara was born, he had been married to a different woman, who died during childbirth. He went on to say that he had raised Mara alone until she was two, when he met and married Joel's mother. "My sister knew that my mother wasn't her natural mother," Joel explains, "but to this day she says my mother was her mother. She never knew any other mother."

His father's revelation did not arouse his curiosity further. Instead, he remembers feeling confusion. "We were a very close family," he says. "For me, the world was a five-block area in Brooklyn and I found it upsetting that suddenly there was this intruder, my sister's mother. Who was this person?"

As time passed, the story receded in importance as he went about the business of growing up. Many years later, his father celebrated his sixty-second birthday and decided to opt for early retirement. Joel drove him to the Social Security insurance office to apply for his benefits. A young woman did the interviewing and when she asked a question, Joel would answer while his father sat and looked on. "I always conducted myself as my father's lawyer," he explains. "I'm not an attorney, but I always answered the questions for him. The interviewer asked where he was born and I answered. Then she asked, 'When did you come to America?' I answered for him. 'When were you naturalized?' So on and so forth. I answered. Then she said, 'How many times have you been married?'

" 'Twice,' I said. My father looks up. He says, 'No, three times.' I say, 'Twice, miss.' He says, 'Miss, may I answer this question? I was married three times.' Was I shocked? Stunned! I was absolutely stunned. I said, 'Do you want to answer the rest of the questions?' He said, 'No, you can continue.'

"She asks, 'How many children do you have?' I answer, 'Three.' My father says, 'No, four.' I was twenty-two years old. I said, 'Excuse me?' He said, 'She asked how many children I had.' I said, 'Is there someone I don't know about?' He said, 'Yes.'

"I don't remember anything about the interviewer's reaction. All I know is I could have fallen to the floor. I was probably the most stunned I have ever been in my entire life."

On the drive home Joel asked his father if he'd like to tell him the story. His father said no, he'd rather not discuss it. The next day, Joel asked his mother and she filled him in.

What Joel learned was that when his father was eighteen years old he had married and had a child, a little girl, and that the marriage was very bad. His mother told him that the woman was "a witch, an evil person," and that his father got a divorce and gave up custody of the child and never saw her again because he wanted to put the whole experience behind him.

Joel found his mother's story disquieting. It seemed inconsistent with his image of his father. Even now, thirty years later and long after both his parents have died, Joel can't accept his mother's version of events.

"Knowing what a warm, compassionate person my father was, something's wrong," he maintains. He cannot believe that his father would give up a child and never see her again. "There's a whole mystery about that part of my father's life that no one can tell me about," he says. "I've talked to my father's surviving sisters and they can't shed any light on it, or they choose not to, or they're very evasive."

One incident in particular convinces Joel that his aunts know more than they let on. The family, following the

Jewish custom, was sitting shiva at his sister Mara's house in New Jersey after Joel's father died. The phone rang, Mara went to answer it, and returned to the room white and shaken. Joel asked her who had called. "I don't remember her name," Mara answered, "but she just called to say she's our sister and to offer her condolences."

He couldn't believe that Mara forgot the caller's name but his sister insisted she was so disoriented by the call that it slipped her memory. Joel wonders how the anonymous caller could have known so quickly of their father's death unless she had been in communication with some member of the family for years.

"To be able to track us down that fast . . . that's very, very strange," he says. "So, I'm certain someone in the family continued to be in touch with this woman who today, my guess is, must be in her sixties."

Although he doesn't know her name and has never heard from his half sister, Joel still would like to meet her.

"Before I went into business," he explains, "I was a very, very good investigator and so people have said to me, 'Why don't you track her down?' But I just never did. I never took the time and I don't know the reason why. I could just go to the Bureau of Vital Statistics in the New York Health Department, go through the records, and find her. At least find a name. But I just haven't ever really felt like doing that."

Perhaps he wonders if his half sister would want to be found and acknowledged. He admits that part of what dissuades him from his search is what happened when his father died.

"That this woman knew who to call, where to call, and yet has always stayed in the shadows. . . ." He adds that he has never been sure how much of what his mother told him about his father's first marriage was fact and how much was fantasy.

Joel continues to think about the secrets, to ponder the questions they raise, and to wonder if he should try to find this woman who calls herself a sister. When he mentions it to people they usually say, "Why bother?" Yet the need to know persists. "I have a feeling that I know this woman from sometime in my childhood," he says, "a family friend, a cousin, something like that. Up until the time I was twelve, I spent a lot of time with my father's side of the family. From then on, it was my mother's side of the family. No particular reason. My mother didn't like this person and that person. My father got along with everyone."

When Joel was about ten years old, on a whim he opened the heavy metal safe in his father's fishmarket when no one was around. He found a bunch of letters inside written to his father by a woman.

"He was having an affair with someone. Basically I understood that," Joel recalls. "Also, I remember picturing this woman in my mind and viewing her as a terrible threat. So what did I do? I brought the letters home to my mother!" He remembers his mother consulting a lawyer and he remembers emotional tumult between his parents, but they never separated and eventually life went on as it had before.

Joel does not recall his father's being angry at him for having snooped and then for having publicized what was obviously a clandestine liaison. One cannot help but wonder at Joel's own capacity to accept and admire his father, frailties, indiscretions, and all. But Joel's father never responded with a heavy hand to his inquisitiveness and the discoveries it wrought, which might explain why Joel never felt the need to judge his father for the content of those discoveries. And so far as he knows, his father never lied to him. When he asked him if he'd like to talk about the information he imparted in the Social Security office, his father simply said, "No, I'd rather not."

"Sometimes I wonder what the reason is for secrecy," he muses. "I respect privacy. I question secrecy. How does one distinguish? I think most things shouldn't be secret, not unless they're in the interest of 'national security,' or one's personal security. Within the parameters of a family, what holds a family together? Love, and caring, and emotional warmth and feeling, as I perceive it. I think that most things should not be secrets. There are some exceptions of course. I think the use of secrecy should be carefully thought out and used only to maintain a family secret that everyone agrees should be secret. When I say everyone, I mean the principles who comprise the secret at the moment."

Yet Joel does not operate under any pretense. Within his own family, he acknowledges that he sometimes stumbles upon secrets being kept from him by his wife and children, "usually revolving around money, or the work ethic, or something that my wife knows would disturb me if I knew about it." From his perspective, his wife conspires with the children in order to protect them from his anger and from the disciplinary measures he might choose to impose. He knows that the children sometimes ally to keep things from their parents or from each other. Yet he is convinced that it's healthier to be open, to be forthright about their failures, wrongdoings, and inadequacies, even at the expense of evoking anger or disappointment. "I've raised my kids to tell the truth and face reality, and if there's something that's disturbing to them, to just say it."

As Joel recalls the day of reckoning at the Social Security office, what he describes is a moment when reality settled in, when he realized that no matter how close he felt to the father whom he adored, there would always be a distance between them. And while he was stunned at the time, he doesn't recall feeling anger. "When I was growing up," he says, "I looked at the world in the following order: there was God, the president of the United States, and my father. That was the chain of command. As I got older, I realized that my father, whom I'd put on this pedestal, was just a mortal man. I came to recognize all his flaws, and loved him just as much."

Laura

From the time she was in high school, Laura Clemmons was aware that her father had relationships with women other than her mother. She recalls a family scene where her mother and father quarreled about it. But her mother decided to stay with him anyhow, not to file for divorce. "We all knew my father went out. We were all aware of it," she explains. "It was part of the acceptance of the family, a problem that everyone in the family knew about. From time to time it occurred to me that there might be another child, but I ignored the thought."

In 1981, Laura's mother, then in her seventies, broke her hip and had to spend time in a rehabilitation center. Candace, Laura's sister, arranged for someone to take care of their mother when she was able to go home. "On the day Candace brought my mother home," Laura says, "my father left her."

Laura, who was overseas on a Peace Corps assignment at the time, returned to the States to find that no one really knew where her father was living. Eventually they discovered that he had moved in with his secretary, a woman named Lesley. Laura had been acquainted with the secretary for a number of years. She knew that Lesley had been separated from her husband for a long time. She also knew that she had a grown daughter who lived with her, and that there were no other children.

Laura was handling some of her father's business affairs at the time her mother was released from the hospital when a problem arose. She needed to get in touch with him so she called the bookkeeper's house and a young man answered the phone. "When I told him I wanted to speak to Lesley," Laura recalls, "he called, 'Mother.' " Some instinct told Laura that this was her father's son.

Laura wasn't worried about protecting her parents' relationship anymore. In fact, she thought that it would be a good idea if her mother considered getting a divorce to protect herself financially. So she told her mother what had happened and said, "I wonder if it's his child?" Her mother dismissed the idea, but Laura persisted. She called her sister and told her and she said, "Of course not, he wouldn't have another child."

When pressed for an explanation, Candace said it must be one of Lesley's boarders, a young person who was particularly fond of her and just called her mother because he liked to. That was plausible. Lesley did rent out rooms. But it still seemed strange.

Several weeks later, Laura spent some time with her father. She is quick to point out that she and her father harbor deep conflicts: there are serious philosophical and political differences, as well as bitterness left over from ill-starred business ventures involving her father and her ex-husband. Laura discovered that her father, then in his eighties, was becoming quite forgetful, although a stranger would be unlikely to notice. Lesley, twenty years younger and very sharp, was pretty much handling his business for him.

As she talked to her father, Laura slipped a seemingly innocuous question into the conversation. "How many children does Lesley have?" she asked. "Two," her father answered, "a son and a daughter." She asked who the boy's father was and he didn't answer. Then she asked if he were the father. He said, "Well, I might be." That was good enough for Laura. She unleashed a whole slew of questions. Some he answered and some he didn't, but she learned enough that she felt certain the boy was his child, her half brother. She went home and told her mother and sister and they both insisted he was kidding, that he didn't have any idea what he was talking about.

By now Laura had to know. She hadn't seen Lesley in a long time but she called her and said she needed to see her to talk about something important. She insisted on meeting her outside the office and alone. They met at a steak house and Laura asked her question straight. There was no denial on Lesley's part, and the truth came out.

"Her son is six months older than my oldest child," Laura says, shaking her head in amazement, "so she and I were pregnant at the same time. My father was having a child and a grandchild within months of each other." The two were born in 1957, and at the time of this meeting they were both twenty-six years old.

"Lesley was a little tense," Laura recalls, "but then I had always felt she didn't like me. We had a courteous relationship but I always felt she was the 'other woman' and I identified with my mother, who was very hurt by this. When I left her after lunch, I had a totally different feeling. I kissed her on the cheek and I said, 'I care about you. You're the mother of my brother.' I didn't feel angry at her. I was fifty at the time. I had seen enough of life's experiences. I don't feel you blame the other woman. It's my father I was angry at." Laura told Lesley that she wanted to meet her half brother—his name was Ken—and Lesley said that she would have him get in touch.

Laura reiterates that the liaison with Lesley wasn't the only relationship her father had outside his marriage. Her father was in real estate and owned a number of buildings. Laura's sister, Candace, had worked for him and she knew, although their mother didn't, that their father kept an apartment for himself in one of the properties. He described it to Candace as a place where he could have some time to himself and unwind, but Candace knew that he also met women there.

"My sister knew more than I did at the time," Laura continues, "and she kept it from my mother and me. She wasn't really given this information. It was what she observed, and she chose not to say anything about it."

Ironically, her father was a very moralistic landlord. If he discovered that there were unmarried men and women living together in his apartments or that there were homosexuals among his tenants, he would try to throw them out. In retrospect, his hypocrisy infuriates Laura and stands as a symbol of the ocean that separates their values.

When Laura returned from the Peace Corps, she and Candace had a heart-to-heart talk about their feelings for their parents. That's when Candace shared what she knew about their father's lifestyle. Although she had long known far more about their father's affairs than did Laura, she didn't want to believe that there was a half brother.

Laura, however, was so eager to meet Ken that she couldn't wait for the young man to get in touch. In the few days that followed her meeting with Lesley, she began to fantasize about what it would be like to have a brother. Her expectations escalated as she grew more excited about the prospect. Her mother and sister, however, were incredulous that she would want to meet this person. They couldn't understand why she couldn't just leave things alone and go on the way they had. Their resistance and disapproval did nothing to deter her.

"I have very ambivalent feelings about my father," Laura says. "There's love but there's also a lot of anger. So uncovering his dereliction wasn't going to stop me from doing what I wanted to do, finding my brother. I wouldn't try to protect him." Ordinarily she might have tried to protect her mother, but under the circumstances she was more convinced than ever that her mother should get a divorce.

"If you're not trying to keep things together," she says, "then you don't care if they explode. I wasn't trying to be destructive, but I had a need to know. I also felt I was going to get something valuable: a brother. As I started finding out more and more, it seemed to me that he was a victim, so I felt positive towards him."

Unable to wait any longer, Laura called Ken. She left a message on his answering machine and Ken returned the call. He was not surprised, because he had known about Laura and Candace all along. The two set a date to meet for lunch and although they hadn't discussed how they would recognize each other, it wasn't a problem. "It was almost a magnetic pull," Laura says. "He looked just like his mother. I was ready to like him. I was ready to tell him anything."

During their lunch what Laura discovered, and what particularly disturbed her, was that Lesley had farmed Ken out with a foster family. She had raised her daughter but she didn't want to upset her own mother by raising an illegitimate child. Ken admitted that he was envious of Candace and Laura, because they had material advantages that he never did. Yet he also said he was grateful that his parents hadn't put him up for adoption, that they saw that he was taken care of. Laura, on the other hand, was incensed. "I'm furious for him," she says. "Why didn't his mother keep him?"

Laura also learned that her father and Lesley had spent Sundays with Ken all during his childhood. On holidays Ken had been given a choice but he had always chosen to stay with his foster parents. When he graduated from high school, he did go to live briefly with Lesley.

As the months passed, Laura continued to be in contact with Ken, but her sister dragged her feet about meeting him. Candace is an actress who appears frequently on TV shows and commercials. Ken had followed her career and was eager to know her. Eventually, at Laura's urging, the three got together for brunch.

Before the meeting Candace pressed Laura not to say anything negative about their father, and she agreed to try. At the brunch Candace asked Ken if their father knew that they were meeting. Ken said that he had told him and that he had responded by saying, "Well, I suppose they'd like to meet the competition."

When her father mentioned competition, Laura explains, he was not referring to feelings of sibling rivalry or the division of parental attention and affection. He was referring to finances and the question of inheritance.

"There's a money problem, which is, of course, stronger than anything else," Laura explains. "Money is very important to Ken. His values are much closer to my father's values than to mine."

At that time, both Candace and Laura felt that Ken was entitled to a child's share of their father's estate when he dies. They thought it fair that he receive the same as they do. In the years that have passed, however, their thinking has changed. Their mother died in 1984, and their father has continued to live with Lesley, who has assumed increasing control over his financial affairs. In the course of untangling a complicated trust agreement involving the distribution of assets in the present, Laura and Candace recently found themselves facing off against their father in a courtroom. The experience changed Laura's opinion of him.

"When we took my father to court," she says, "he was so sweet. He hugged and kissed us and I started to realize that maybe we hadn't recognized how confused he was and how badly his memory served him."

It is ironic that Laura, who looked at Ken as "a gift," now finds that she and Ken no longer speak to each other. What happened is that her father's lawyer called a meeting to discuss financial matters. Laura attended and Lesley went too. After the meeting, Laura called Ken to report on the discussion since it also affected him. Ken was furious that he hadn't been invited to attend. In his anger, he jumped to false conclusions and accused Laura of being dishonest and of purposefully excluding him from the session. "I didn't arrange that meeting," Laura observes. "But I did attend because my lawyer suggested I go to it. And then I even called Ken and told him about it."

Candace continues to keep in touch with Ken through telephone conversations. It is clear that there are formidable legal hassles still ahead. Laura also spent enough time with Ken to become aware of his excessive drinking. She now says quietly, "I think he's got some serious problems."

The difference in values and the financial competition make it difficult to envision a storybook ending to Laura's story. It is doubtful that she will find in Ken the kind of relationship she wished for, perhaps unrealistically.

Laura's sense of fairness shows in her statement that Ken is her father's child as much as she and Candace. Yet it is that same sense of fairness that embitters her toward Ken. If Lesley inherits the lion's portion of the estate and the three children share equally, much of Lesley's share presumably will be passed on to Ken.

Under such convoluted circumstances, one wonders whether the relationship between Laura and her half brother would have fared better had she known of him earlier. Laura believes it would have. The biggest difference would have been that Ken was included in the family, not cast aside. They would have had the opportunity to develop a history of experiences together, and perhaps that would have tempered the animosity and harsh feelings that have developed around the inheritance.

Laura never thought her father was a totally honest person, and when she first learned about Ken she felt as though nothing her father said "was worth listening to." Yet as the story continues to unfold, she wonders if even now she really knows the truth.

Like so many others who have felt deceived by information kept from them in their families, Laura's pain is rooted more in the act of concealment than in the content of the secret. While she deplored the way her father treated her mother, she knew about his behavior all along. It did not form the content of the family secret. That content, she thought until recently, was the existence of Ken. Now she wonders if she is twice duped.

Perhaps the secret is that her father's faculties have been deteriorating for much longer than she realized. Maybe he really meant it when Laura first asked him if he were Ken's father and he said, "Well, I might be."

Even when pressed, her father only half grudgingly acknowledged that Ken was indeed his child, further exacerbating Laura's conflicted feelings about him. It was only through her own insistence, by confronting Lesley directly and then by aggressively pursuing contact with Ken, that Laura was able to fit the pieces of her family puzzle together. She didn't get much help, even after the skeleton had tumbled out of the closet.

Today she is left wondering if the secret is that Ken is really her half brother or if the secret is that her father's mistress has hatched a plot worthy of a steamy novel. "Maybe," she says, "the most important secret is that my father has been mentally incompetent for over ten years and my sister and I never knew it."

Daniel

When Daniel Rosenthal was thirteen, a young man in his early twenties came to live with Daniel's family. As far as Daniel knew, this young man, Aaron, was a distant cousin without parents of his own who moved from one set of relatives to another.

Having grown up without a stable family, Aaron was used to taking care of himself. He couldn't abide the house rules that Nathaniel Rosenthal, Daniel's father, imposed, like restrictions on how late he could stay out at night. The two fought constantly. To make matters worse, Daniel's mother, Elena, didn't want this outsider in the house and did all she could to prevent her husband and Aaron from resolving their conflicts. The climate in the house, turbulent to begin with, grew stormy, with fights at nearly every meal.

"When Aaron showed up," Daniel remembers, "he was just someone living in our house. I don't think it was ever really explained to me who he was." Aaron, however, was the spitting image of Nathaniel. He looked much more like the senior Rosenthal than did Daniel.

Perhaps it was because of this physical likeness, perhaps because of innuendos he heard from his aunts and uncles, but for whatever reason, Daniel soon sensed that there was a deeper, more specific relationship between his father and Aaron than he had been told. But, reluctant to risk further upsetting the already volatile atmosphere in the house, he never asked for clarification. Then too, Aaron only stayed for a period of months. When he left, Daniel pretty much stopped thinking about him, grateful that a modicum of peace was restored to his home.

Several years later, Aaron resurfaced. He began to make claims on Nathaniel, and Daniel's relatives made it clear that they felt Nathaniel owed Aaron something. It was then, for the first time, that Nathaniel told Daniel that he had been married in the old country, that his wife had been unfaithful to him, and that Aaron was the product of that unfaithfulness, the son of his wife's lover. Acknowledging that Daniel would hear from other relatives that Aaron was his son, Nathaniel said emphatically, "I want you always to remember that he is *not* my son.' " For Daniel, his father's revelations were only a beginning. From his relatives, he learned more.

The Rosenthal family secret germinated in Russia more than seventy years ago. Nathaniel, a Russian Jew who married very young, arrived home one day to find his wife in bed with another man. His wife gave birth to a male child in the months that followed and he insisted the baby was the product of this illicit union. He never acknowledged the child and he immediately divorced his wife.

"In the shtetls, the small villages in Europe at the time, Jews weren't allowed any place in court," Daniel explains. "They couldn't be married in the eyes of the court because they had no standing. They were not citizens. They were not allowed to own land. So my father was married by Jewish law, and the divorce law with Orthodox Jews is that the male may divorce his wife at any time by simply saying, 'I divorce thee.' "

Daniel is not certain whether the marriage had ended by the time the baby was born. Subsequently his father immigrated to America and married his second wife, Elena, Daniel's mother. Several years after he relocated, he paid to have the child he had disowned brought to this country. He did it because his brothers back in Russia threatened to pay the child's way if he didn't, and he was too proud to let them do that. He said, "No, if he's coming to this country, I'm going to pay for it because his mother was my wife." The boy, Aaron, went to live with Nathaniel's sister and mother, in the same city that the rest of the extended family lived in, just down the street from Nathaniel and his new family.

Daniel was in his early twenties and married himself by the time he was really able to understand what had happened and to fathom the enormity of the rejection that Aaron experienced.

In the years that followed, he and his wife made a purposeful effort to bring Aaron into their family, ignoring Nathaniel's displeasure. "He was uncle to my children," Daniel explains, "and we would have him to our house weekends and whenever he had a vacation.

"My father," Daniel continues, "was most unhappy about the fact that I maintained a relationship with Aaron throughout the years. But he was a very kind and loving man otherwise so naturally he forgave me."

Innovative, smart, and determined, Daniel's father came to this country intent on realizing the American dream. "He needed to become a millionaire," Daniel explains, "not because the money meant anything to him, but because it was the most important thing he could do to show his power and success in life." Nathaniel's pursuit of his dream began in a shoe factory, which is also where he met his second wife, Elena.

Nathaniel made good on his dream, if only briefly. He became a footwear manufacturer and developed a method of turning out shoes for ninety-five cents a pair, using assembly line methods. He started out in Boston and then moved to the suburb of Marlboro, where the city built him a factory. Within six months, he had six hundred people working for him.

In a period of about seven years, the business blossomed, boomed, and went defunct, a victim of the rash of sit-down strikes that hit the country in 1932, combined with the importation of less expensive shoes from Czechoslovakia, where labor was much cheaper.

A millionaire on paper in 1930, Nathaniel Rosenthal lost everything in 1932. After that, he borrowed enough money to open a small cigar store in Boston. From that point on, until Nathaniel's death in the mid 1940s, Daniel and his wife deposited $100 a month in the senior Rosenthal's bank account. That, plus Social Security and the meager profits pulled from the store, was enough for an elderly couple to live on.

"Eventually," Daniel says, "I insisted that my father write a will. So we went to the lawyer and his only provision was that Aaron not get one single dime of his money, nothing." He died at eighty, leaving $10,000, most of which came from Daniel, and a house which Daniel had bought him.

"Ten thousand dollars wouldn't go very far," Daniel continues, "but I was their only child and my mother was my responsibility, and I didn't mind that." His mother continued to live in her house and Daniel made sure her needs were met.

Aaron, however, was distraught. He was convinced that his father had died a wealthy man and that he must have had some money socked away somewhere. He thought that he would inherit at least $50,000 and was incredulous that there was nothing for him. "The lawyer," Daniel recalls, "was kind enough not to tell him, 'He specifically left you nothing.' "

When he was about forty, Aaron moved to California. "He was very bitter," Daniel recalls. "He lived a kind of nomadic, unstructured existence, spent much of his life at the racetrack, and married a woman to whom he was most unkind."

After Nathaniel died, Daniel and his wife visited Aaron in California to try to ameliorate some of his bitterness, but found it futile. "I said to him," Daniel remembers, " 'If it were up to me, I'd give you the $10,000, but it was left in my care for my mother.' " Aaron refused to be placated.

Malcontented and dissatisfied, Aaron fleeced his wife and left her. He later married a woman with a daughter, who was thrown out of the house when she was about sixteen. Aaron had a child of his own by his second wife, a son whom he abused. "Aaron was very bitter all his life," Daniel observes, "and it's understandable. To have a father who makes you a family secret . . ."

Aaron died of lung cancer when he was in his early sixties.

3

My Mother's Other Child

W E may love our brothers and sisters, we may hate them. We may be close or distant, sympathetic or antagonistic. Whatever we feel toward our siblings, they influence who and what we are. We share the same parents, the same genetic inheritance. Our siblings balance our families of origin. They increase the facets of our identity by conferring on us a new role beyond that of son or daughter, for we cannot be a brother or a sister unless we have a brother or sister of our own.

We may vie with siblings for our parents' attention, we may silently wish for them to fail, to get into trouble, to get out of the limelight. Sometimes we worship and idolize an older brother or sister. Sometimes we interpret our own role of brother or sister as surrogate parent, taking care of the younger ones. However we color the role, as ally, enemy, or co-conspirator, the fact that we have, and therefore are, a sibling helps define our position in the family and our sense of self. That's why discovering an unknown sibling in adulthood can shake up our assumptions about who we are and where we fit in.

When we think of adoption and the issue of secrecy, most of us focus on the secret that forms when a child's adoptive parents pretend that the child is their natural offspring and do not tell him or her of the adoption. But for every such case there is a corollary secret, one that is probably even more common. In this instance, it is the natural mother who makes a secret of the baby whom she gave up for adoption.

Kim and Sandy

Kim Morris is in his mid thirties. His story begins in a New England industrial city where he grew up with his mother and a brother four years his senior. He also had regular though infrequent contact with a half brother, fourteen years older than he. Today he and his mother and brothers all live within several hours' drive of each other in Massachusetts and New Hampshire.

Kim's mother, Martha, married very young and had a son, Kim's oldest brother, James. She divorced her husband, remarried, and then had Mark. Four years after that, Kim was born.

Martha divorced again, and later, when Kim was eight, married a third time, to the man Kim calls his stepfather. Kim had always been led to believe that the second husband, Mark's father, was his father as well. This man disappeared from the scene when Kim was very young, perhaps even before he was born, and Kim never met him.

Kim's childhood was marked by not enough money and too much upheaval. His mother and stepfather changed jobs frequently, and often fought with each other. "We didn't have a great, solid life," Kim explains. "My mother and stepfather were both heavy drinkers and all that goes with that. So we moved around a lot."

There is no grief in Kim's voice when he says that his stepfather is dead now. In fact, he always felt that his stepfather was an outsider, a threat to the core of his family. Like a wounded child who does not want to reveal too much of his pain, he says quietly that he felt that his family was the three of them—he and his mother and his brother Mark. "The only father figure I ever had," he adds, "was my grandfather, my mother's father, and he died when I was thirteen."

Although Kim knew that his background formed a geneologist's nightmare, he learned only recently that there were even more branches on the family tree than he ever imagined. About a year ago, he and his wife went on a rafting trip with Mark and some friends. Kim drove the two hours to his mother's house to drop off his two children for the weekend.

When he got back to work a few hours later, his mother called him. She told him she wanted to talk with him about something when he got back, adding that, "it's nothing bad."

Kim knew that something important was coming up because it was totally out of character for Martha to call him at work. He owns his own graphic design business, which he oversees from a complex of offices and studio space housed in a restored mill building. Martha is impressed and perhaps a little intimidated by his accomplishments, and is careful not to intrude.

At the end of the weekend Kim drove to his mother's to pick up his children. After he hugged the kids, they went off to play and Martha told him what was on her mind.

She related the events to him chronologically and he found his mind racing ahead, trying to finish the story. "She told me she had been pregnant between Mark and me, and first I thought she was going to tell me she had an abortion. She got through that and then I saw that wasn't it. I began to think she was going to end up telling me I was adopted and I started to think, 'How am I going to deal with this?' "

Then Martha told him that while she was married to her second husband, Mark's father, she had begun what was to become a five-year-long affair with a married man, the owner of a small restaurant. During this time she separated from Mark's father and became pregnant, eventually giving birth to a daughter. Already struggling to feed James and Mark, she moved in with her own mother and arranged to have the baby adopted. Several years later, the same man fathered Kim. Her life had calmed down by that point, and she was able to keep the baby boy.

"By the time she got to the crux of it, I was sort of in shock," Kim says. "She told me that I have a sister, Sandy. 'I have a sister?' My first reaction was laughter. I was numb. I was more excited at the idea of having a sister than anything else."

During the two-hour-long ride home from his mother's house, however, his initial euphoria began to dissipate. Doubts and grievances took its place. "I started thinking about how much we'd missed," he says, "and wondering how everyone could have lied to us for so long. The basis of any relationship is trust, particularly the relationship with your parents—believing they're telling you the truth. So by the time I got home I was pretty much a wreck." He told his wife and then together they told their kids. Kim spent the next few days taking long walks and crying a lot.

The unveiling of his family secret, that he had a sister, rocked Kim's every notion of his own identity. It was a secret that bred other secrets, for he also discovered that his brother Mark was indeed his half-brother.

"I felt as though I'd gained a sister and lost a brother at the same time," Kim explains. He discovered too that the man he had thought was his father was not his father at all. Instead, his father was a man he had never even heard of before.

Although the news of his sister Sandy's existence and the revelations that accompanied it jolted him like an emotional earthquake, Kim now remembers that as he was growing up there were hints that something was not quite as it appeared. "There were inconsistencies," he recalls. "Both Mark and I had the name of our mother's first husband, not her second husband, whom we'd been told was our father. We were told that she went back to her first married name after the divorce from our father, so we didn't question that. It sort of made sense."

Then he remembered once in his twenties, at a time when he found himself having difficulty in his personal life, he had thought about trying to find his natural father. His mother had been reluctant to help him. "What she did," he says, "was to give me information about the man who I thought was my father (her second husband), so in fact I could have gone on this wild goose chase, hunting down this man who wasn't my father anyway."

Why had he never been told the truth? And why was the secret of Sandy's existence being shared with him only now?

In her mid thirties, Sandy is married and lives in the Chicago area. Several years ago she gave birth to a stillborn baby. The experience evoked difficult feelings about her own beginnings.

Leaving the hospital without her baby, feeling depressed and sad, she felt a need to understand how her own mother, Martha, could have chosen to leave the hospital empty-armed when Sandy herself was born. Sandy joined an adoption support group in an effort to deal with her concerns. She decided she wanted to find her real mother, not to make any claims on her, but just to let her know that she thought about her. Sandy began to pursue her past, searching through court dockets until her adoption decree finally surfaced. The document lists the name of the baby's mother and of the person who adopted her. Sandy found it a strange coincidence that her birth mother's surname and her adoptive surname were the same. The two women were, in fact, cousins.

Sandy's adoptive mother, Ann, lived in Chicago at the time Sandy was conceived. She very much wanted a child but had been plagued by a series of miscarriages. So when her cousin, Martha, became pregnant once again they made a pact with each other. Martha would give her baby to Ann, and they would never communicate with each other again. Martha went to Chicago where Ann and her husband took care of her until the baby was born, gave her daughter up for adoption at birth, and returned back East to put the experience behind her. Throughout the nearly thirty years that followed, she honored the pact and made no contact with either her cousin or her daughter. It was Sandy who initiated the reunion.

Sandy is quick to point out that she grew up knowing that she was adopted. The secret, from her perspective, revolved around the identity of her natural family. Unlike many adoptees, however, Sandy's adoptive parents obviously knew a great deal about her biological parents.

There were times during Sandy's childhood when she would ask her adoptive mother questions about her origins and Ann would say, "Well, I can't really tell you very much about your real mother, except that she was very young and she gave you away because she couldn't take care of you."

As Sandy became more deeply involved in trying to untangle her past, working through the resources of the adoption support group, she decided to turn to Ann for information one last time.

"I wrote her a letter," Sandy recalls, "and told her what I already knew and that I was really serious about this. I told her that I wasn't going to be looking for another mother but that I just wanted to know what my history was, for myself and for my children. She called me up and said, 'Well, you're thirty years old and I guess you have a right to know.' She told me that my mother was her first cousin and that she had been trying to have a baby herself. Then she told me that I had an older half brother. Then she said, 'Are you really going to pursue this? It's probably best to leave it as it is.' Afterwards she added, 'If you're going to go further, you should probably do it through your older brother.' Finally she said, 'I just broke a promise I made thirty years ago.' "

Ann gave Sandy her brother's name and described the area in Massachusetts where she thought James might live. After checking with directory information in several towns, Sandy was able to find his telephone number. "I called once and he wasn't home," she recalls, "and I didn't have the courage to call again. If he wasn't home, well maybe that meant that was the way it was supposed to be."

Sandy's husband became very frustrated with her for giving up, however, and the next day, when she was out of the house, he made the call for her. "He got James on the phone," she says, "and laid the whole thing out on the table.

"James was very open," she continues. "Nothing really surprised him, maybe because he hadn't been very close to his family. He wanted to exchange letters and phone calls, and then about six months later I flew out to Boston and met him. When I saw him, all I could think was here's finally somebody that I look like, somebody I really resemble."

For about four years, he was the only contact she had with her family. James gave her their mother's address and told her about Kim and Mark, but at first she didn't follow up because, she explains, "I didn't want James to feel I was using him to get to the rest of the family. I wanted to establish a relationship with him and I didn't want to cause any trouble."

Eventually she decided to write to her natural mother. She sent a chatty, newsy letter that said she was happy, described her family, and said that if Martha wanted to make contact, she was ready and willing. As it happened, James had already told Martha about Sandy's efforts.

Sandy never did get an answer to her first letter. "From what I had heard about her reaction when James told her about me, that's what I'd expected," Sandy explains. "She was shocked and terrified. She wasn't ready to deal with all the secrets that she'd put behind her."

Sandy continued her relationship with James and in December of 1988, on a whim, she sent her mother a Christmas card, along with a brief note and a picture of her family. "It was unassuming," she says. "I didn't ask her to answer me. I didn't ask for anything."

The same day that Sandy mailed the card, James called and said he had gotten a note from their mother and that she had asked for Sandy's address.

"The same day I sent my card," she murmurs, struck by the coincidence. "So I told him this is really strange, because I just wrote her." Sandy did get a card from Martha and the two began exchanging letters. They were newsy at first, but as winter softened to spring, they became more open with each other. But there still was no telephone contact.

Then in May a strange thing happened. A woman from the "Oprah Winfrey Show" called Sandy and said that she had gotten her name from the adoption support group and that they were putting a show together for Mother's Day, where children would be reunited with their natural mothers on the show. She said, "Would you like to do that?" And Sandy answered, "I don't know. I've never even spoken to her on the phone." The woman said that she would make the call for Sandy. Sandy got the number from James and called the show back. Then she wished she hadn't. Since her brothers were still in the dark, reuniting on national television didn't seem like a good idea. She decided to call Martha herself.

"That was the first time I ever talked to her," she recalls. "Toward the end, I started crying—because she got emotional. She told me how much she cherished my letters and photographs. And then she said, 'I can't wait to meet the children.' I said 'Really? You mean you'll come here?' And she said, 'Yes,' and I couldn't believe it. It was something that I had wanted but I hadn't pressured her into it. It was her idea."

At the end of the conversation Martha said, "I'll be telling Kim and Mark about you, but I just don't know how I'll do it."

Sandy called her on Mother's Day and Martha told her that she had shared the secret with Mark and that he had accepted it and been happy. Then she said, "But it's really going to be difficult to tell Kim. He's your full brother and he thinks Mark is his full brother. I don't know how I'm going to do this but he's coming by tomorrow and I've got to do it."

"I felt so bad for her," Sandy recalls. "I felt so frustrated. She was really taking a chance, that he could be bitter towards her." A few weeks later Sandy came home to find a message waiting. Kim had called.

Sitting in his office three months after learning of his sister's existence, Kim takes up the story.

"One of the things that hurts most about this," he reflects, "is that on both my mother's side and her cousin's side, this promise they made to each other was sacred above all else. It was really the only thing that mattered to them, not what was best for everybody involved. Just recently, we found out that the only three people in the family who didn't know about Sandy were me and my brothers. My maternal grandparents knew, my aunts and uncles and my cousins and their spouses knew. It wasn't just a secret between two people. There were a lot of people involved, so I feel a lot of bitterness there."

For her part, Sandy even knew her biological grandparents, who were also Kim's grandparents, but who, when they came to Chicago to visit, were identified to her as Uncle Harold and Aunt Mary. Kim, who was largely brought up by these grandparents, notes that there are photographs of him and his grandparents together and there are also photographs of them with Sandy, their "niece," in Chicago. He and his sister were related through adoption as well as through blood.

In the years since Sandy first contacted James, Kim explains, "My oldest half brother and my sister developed a relationship where they'd visit each other back and forth. But there was a limit to how close they could get. Sandy's very affectionate and James isn't." Still no one had told Kim of Sandy's existence.

"James continued the secret," Kim says, "and that was partly my sister's doing. James had never really been part of our lives, so my sister dealt with it in the only right way for us. She felt Mark and I had to learn about her from our mother."

What adds to Kim's frustration is that during these years, Sandy was getting more and more information piled on her. Each new discovery created more questions and doubts, further diminishing her self-worth, already bruised by the knowledge that her natural mother had given her up and by the way her adoptive parents treated her.

"My sister wasn't abused," he says, "but she wasn't treated very well emotionally. Her parents eventually had a son of their own and he became their prize and she became their adopted daughter. When they introduced their children, it would be, 'This is our son Charles and this is our adopted daughter Sandy,' so it became sort of a qualification of her existence. She had to change her wedding date because her brother had a football game.

"When she heard our mother had three sons," Kim continues, "two older and one younger than she, she wondered, 'Why me?' And her mother, Ann, said, 'Well Martha just doesn't like girls.' But the agreement was made before she was born, so our mother didn't know whether it would be a boy or a girl anyway."

When Martha finally told Kim about Sandy, she intimated that if she hadn't been able to arrange for her cousin to adopt the baby, she probably would have had an illegal abortion. She told him how through the years she had fantasized that her daughter had a good upbringing and a more stable environment than she was able to provide her sons. And in fact, says Kim, Sandy did have a more predictable family structure, but a lot less emotional support than he and his brother. "We didn't have a very secure life," he says, talking about himself and Mark, "but we at least knew that our mother loved us very much and that she would do anything for us."

Through the creation of their shared secret and their promise to erase one another from their lives, Martha and Ann participated in a complicity which not only denied Kim a sister, but also denied him accurate knowledge of his own origins. In addition, they convoluted his relationship with his half brother Mark.

For four years, Sandy knew about Kim and Mark, but they didn't know about her. Even when Martha decided she would have to tell the boys, Kim, who is considered the family success, was told several weeks after Mark, a fact which Kim still finds disconcerting. "She worried about my reaction. She worried that I would reject her," Kim explains.

At the time of the rafting trip, the weekend that Martha took care of Kim's children, Martha had already told Mark about Sandy. Yet Mark said nothing to Kim, and at this point Kim doesn't blame him. According to Kim, "It just had to come from my mother because any bitterness I had would have been compounded if it didn't. Then I'd have to go to her and say, 'Why didn't you tell me?' But I don't think my brother would have let it go on much longer. In fact, he kept telling my mother, 'You've got to tell Kim. You've got to tell him.' " Right after the trip, of course, Martha did tell him. Later that same day, Kim wrote Sandy a letter, not a terribly deep letter he says, because after all, "She came looking for her mother, not for me."

But as soon as he sent the letter he found himself becoming increasingly agitated. He thought about Sandy constantly and found himself going on long walks and just crying. "The negative aspects were just consuming me," he reflects, "what we missed, the deceit."

The day after Kim mailed his letter, he couldn't stand the tension anymore. He decided he couldn't wait, that he would call her. Sandy wasn't home and she ended up calling him back.

"We had no idea what we were going to say to each other," he remembers. "Well, there were about five seconds of uneasiness and then there was this immediate bond."

He decided he needed to go to Chicago right away. "That's really why I called," he says, "because I wanted to go there. I felt like I'd had to wait in line to know about her." His mother had told him that Sandy planned a trip east the following month, but he didn't want to wait until then because he didn't want to share her with his mother and brothers all at the same time. "I felt I needed to go out there and have some time alone with her, to get to know her a little personally."

Sandy met him at the airport and they recognized each other immediately. As Kim explains, "It's like we knew each other inside out almost right away."

They held hands as they walked to Sandy's car. "It was almost a physical thing," Kim marvels. "Almost like a part of our bodies had been reunited or reattached somehow, like we were Siamese twins who had been separated and were now back together again and felt much better about it."

In the long talks that followed, they discovered how similar they were in their values and feelings. When it was time for Kim to leave, the pain was, as he describes it, excruciating, a reaction to their good-byes which persists even now, a year and many visits later.

"When we leave each other," he says, "we have these identical physical reactions. An intense pain in the chest and we can't breath. It's almost overwhelming."

In trying to describe how he feels about finding his sister, Kim says, "Having a child, that's all I can compare it with. There was that immediate love and acceptance. We're both perfect. We'd never do anything wrong, we'd never hurt each other. Even now, when she tells me about her painful experiences, it hurts as if she were my own child."

Perhaps because she had always felt herself something of a second-class citizen in the family she grew up with, Sandy had protected herself from disappointment by minimizing her expectations. She imagined that Kim would react to knowledge of her existence with apathy, maybe mild curiosity. "I never expected someone to hop on a plane and come out and meet me," she muses. "I wasn't brought up with that kind of self-confidence."

When Kim assesses the aftermath of his family secret, he cannot help but catalog his regrets. He is angry that he was kept apart from the person he now feels closest to. He is angry too that he was not able to be there to comfort Sandy during the low period in her life when she and her husband were having difficulties and she suffered the loss of the baby which ultimately spurred her to search for her birth mother.

"She literally felt alone," he says, "and it's so frustrating to know that the reason I couldn't be there for her was because it was convenient to continue the secret."

Kim regrets too that he has missed knowing Sandy's children as they've grown up. His nieces and his nephew and his own two sons are part of the reason he continues to be haunted by the four lost years between the time Sandy contacted James and Martha and the time he discovered her. He reasons that while he and his sister are probably not so different from what they were several years ago, their children have changed enormously, and he is saddened by all that he has missed of their lives. It is as though he wants to make up for lost time by lavishing his attention and affection on them, particularly the oldest, Sandy's fourteen-year-old daughter, whom he feels a particular urgency to know. He writes to each child individually and they write to him too.

As part of its legacy, the secret has also affected his relationship with his mother.

"It bothers me that she wouldn't trust me enough to know that I wouldn't desert her because of this," he says. Yet he has tried to contain his anger because he reasons that "lashing out would just confirm her fears and prove that she was right, that she never should have told me."

The day his mother told him about Sandy, Kim asked if there was anything else she wanted to tell him. He said it jokingly but as it turned out, there was more Martha wanted to say. She told him his real father's name and that both he and she had been married to others at the time Kim was conceived.

When he returned home later that same day, Kim wrote his mother a long letter sharing his feelings, but he didn't send it because he thought it would cause her too much anguish. Thinking back, he says he wasn't ready yet to bare those emotions to her. Recently, however, he did write to her, explaining that what hurts him most is the four years between the time Sandy contacted her and the time she told him the secret.

"I didn't want to put a whole lot more guilt on her than she already had," he says, "but I needed to let her know how I felt. From my perspective, my sister is a miracle that I was deprived of for a long time."

Currently Kim and Sandy write four or five letters a week to each other, in addition to frequent lengthy phone calls. "Our letters tend to deal 80% in emotions," Kim reflects, as though they both had an unmet need to share strong feelings. Sandy continues to be astounded by Kim's warmth.

"She commented to me in a letter recently that we're so much alike that by loving me so much, she feels better about herself. If you suddenly see yourself in someone else and you feel they're a pretty good person, there are a lot of positive things that come out of that." When they're together they stay up until two or three in the morning, after everyone else has gone off to bed. "We don't even say that much," Kim reflects. "We'll just kind of be together, hug and physically be together.

"We're pretty much mirrors of each other," he continues, "physically and otherwise. Our feelings about things, the way we raise our children. We both converted to Catholicism in the same year. We were both raised largely by our separate grandmothers, and as we look back, we both have the same feeling, like they were our mothers."

"Basically who I am and what I've learned, I've gotten from my grandparents," Sandy affirms. Both her adoptive parents worked, and when they weren't working they were heavily involved in her brother Charles's activities. Sandy's grandfather traveled frequently, and consequently she spent a lot of time alone with her grandmother.

"Kim and I have the same needs," Sandy continues. "This need to belong, to be wanted and needed, and to take care of people. We both feel we have a kindred spirit now."

Kim recognizes that breaking a secret doesn't always have as happy an ending as in his experience. He notes that one of the things adoption support groups do is to prepare you for outright rejection. Not surprisingly, birth mothers react in a great variety of ways when contacted by the children they gave up long ago.

"Sandy was already feeling very unwanted, which was part of the reason she started to look for her mother," Kim explains. "To subject yourself to the possibility of that sort of rejection is a big risk."

Sandy believes the story has given her a fresh perspective, a keener appreciation of all her family, both in Chicago and in Massachusetts. She has always encouraged her children to treat each other with respect, and she has tried to help them understand that there may be times in their lives when the only friends they have are their brother and sisters. While school and neighborhood friends come and go, family is always there.

"A lot of times," she says, "I'll watch my children together and I'll think this is what we could have had, this is what it would have been like. I just think that if we'd been brought up together, we would have been very close. For me, that's a loss, that we missed that." Yet Sandy also acknowledges that part of the reason she and Kim find each other so in harmony may be that they don't have to contend with the frustration, hurt, and envy that are predictable ingredients in a shared childhood.

For Martha and Ann, breaking the secret has involved reestablishing contact, churning up a volatile emotional history. It has also put stress on their relationship with their grown children. Ann cannot help but feel threatened by Martha's new part in Sandy's life.

Kim's wife sometimes becomes frustrated by the all-absorbing nature of Sandy and Kim's relationship. As Kim explains it, initially his wife was as excited as he was at discovering Sandy. "But I think that my having a sister has become normal for her over a period of time, that the intensity has worn off, which it hasn't for me. Now I've gotten to the point where I don't think this is ever going to be normal."

According to Sandy, Ann and Martha are having a parallel experience. About a month after Kim flew to Chicago to meet her for the first time, Sandy and Ann came east to get together with the whole family: Martha, her three sons, and their wives and children. While the visit went smoothly for a couple of days, eventually the two mothers started sniping at each other.

"I think that the intensity of the emotion between Kim and me just got to be too much for them," Sandy speculates.

One unexpected result of Sandy's emergence has been a lessened distance between James and everyone else.

"The night of the reunion," Kim recalls, "is the first time I can ever remember having a conversation with James other than 'How are you? What have you been doing?'

That night we went off and had maybe a five-minute conversation about his life. Our mother once had a rather adventurous lifestyle and he had grown up with it. He had been aware of it. By the time Mark and I came along, she had settled down a lot. I could never understand how he had turned out so different from us when he had the same upbringing we had. But in fact he didn't, and there's a lot of pain there." Although James still has not re-entered the family fold, that possibility seems open now.

For Sandy, the discovery of her family and of Kim in particular has confirmed her ideas about how to raise her own children. It has also had a healing effect on her lifelong conflict with her adoptive brother, Charles, who has had his share of problems.

Sandy's adoptive parents moved to Florida a few years ago. When Sandy visited them she found out that her brother was serving a prison sentence on a drunk driving charge—her parents hadn't told her. She visited him in jail and when she got home, she wanted to talk about her experiences with her family, but she didn't tell her own children because her parents didn't want her to. Ann even wanted Sandy to forward all letters to the prison through her, lessening the chance that her grandchildren would figure out where their uncle was.

At that point, Sandy said she couldn't cooperate because she felt she was being dishonest with her older children. Finally she told Ann, "Mom, I can't lie to these kids. They understand about drugs and alcohol. This might be a lesson for them. And they love him too." So Ann had to agree.

When her brother got out of jail, Sandy made another trip south. She had found her last visit degrading for both of them, and it was important to her to be there for him at a time when he was putting his life back together. Charles knew about her efforts to find her birth relatives and was curious about what was happening. Sandy brought along a brief videotape Kim had made, a sentimental collage of photographs of him and Sandy, their parents, grandparents, and brothers, now and when they were younger, and she offered to show it to Charles, making it easy for him to refuse if he felt uncomfortable. "He made me run it three times," she remembers, "and then he said to me, 'Sandy, you've always been special but I never told you that.' "

Karl

"I was an only child until I was twenty-four," Karl Arland quips, his voiced tinged with sarcasm. Then his mother told him she had given up a daughter for adoption two years before he was born.

"It was around Christmas time," he says, recalling the moment at which his mother disclosed her secret. He had been feeling depressed and wanted to ignore Christmas, and his mother had agreed to his request that they skip the presents this year. "Then she showed up with a tractor trailer full of gifts," he says, shaking his head. "After I opened them all up, it was like, well, here's one other thing. So she told me about Olivia. I refer to it as the Christmas I received an older sister."

When his mother, Lisette, was seventeen and fresh out of high school, she spent the summer working at a beach resort where she had an affair with a man ten years older than she. She got pregnant and gave birth to a daughter, who was immediately put up for adoption. Twenty-six years later the two were reunited at the daughter's initiative.

"It was something that I had had to live with by myself for all those years, without sharing it," Lisette explains. "My mother was the only member of the family that knew."

Lisette was the second youngest of five children in a working-class rural New Hampshire family that was always on the edge of poverty. Her parents, she says, were unsophisticated about the world outside their small town. When she became pregnant, her mother wanted her to have the baby and keep it and continue living at home, but Lisette wanted to break out of her family cycle. She felt that following her mother's inclinations would have meant giving up her chance to make a richer life for herself.

She was also determined that her baby would have a better childhood than she herself had known. She wanted her baby to be part of a family that wanted her and that would be financially and emotionally able to care for her, and she trusted that the adoption agency would make a good choice. "I wasn't in any position to raise a child," she says, "and even though my mother really wanted the baby at home, especially after Olivia was born on her birthday, I didn't want her bringing this child up. It just wasn't an environment that I wanted a child of mine to be in. I didn't want her to go through what I went through. I didn't have much guidance. I didn't have communication. I didn't have knowledge. I didn't get any of those things from my family because they didn't have them to give.

"I always had clothes and food and I was always warm," she adds, explaining that her own mother had lived in an orphanage, "cold and hungry," from the age of nine to fifteen because her widowed father and older siblings didn't want her.

"I didn't blame my mother for seeing food and clothes as the end all and be all. I just didn't want it to go on for another generation. I thought the best thing for the baby was to allow her to be adopted. And I wanted to do something with my own life."

Lisette remembers clearly the morning her mother asked her if she were pregnant. "I cried and cried," she says, adding, "My mother wasn't angry. All my life, whenever I was in trouble, she felt closer to me. When everything was going well, she felt as though I had no need for her, and she needed to be needed."

She had been dating a boy from a neighboring town early in her teens and had become very close to his family. In fact, she would eventually marry one of his brothers.

"It was a very bizarre household, but I was always there and I always felt comfortable," she remembers. It was the mother in that family, Lucy Arland, who arranged for Lisette to go to the Florence Crittendon Hastings House for Unwed Mothers in Boston to await the birth and adoption of her child.

Lisette had graduated from high school and was working as a secretary in a law office at the time. She lived at home but spent considerable time at the Arland's house, where she became close friends with the oldest son, Ethan, newly returned from a stint in the service.

"He asked me how it happened," she remembers, "but instead of making me feel like a bad girl, which is how I already felt, he started helping me deal with it, which is probably the reason I fell in love with him."

When she was six months pregnant, Lisette entered the Florence Crittendon Home. "At the time," she says, "I had no idea how fortunate I was to be able to go to this elite unwed mothers home, where the care was excellent. There were about thirty other girls there, mostly from wealthier backgrounds. Theoretically you had to have money to go there, but they had some allowance for people who didn't and Lucy Arland got me in."

Lisette's own family, with the exception of her mother, thought that she had taken a job in Boston and to them "Boston was a million miles away from New Hampshire." While many women look back on a home for unwed mothers as a miserable chapter in their lives, for Lisette the experience was exhilarating.

"It was a wonderful time for me," she says. "It was like boarding school. I learned to play bridge. I was exposed to rooms filled with Oriental rugs and English furniture. It was another lifestyle, unlike anything I'd known."

Ethan visited her twice at the home, and he came with her mother to pick her up when it was time to go back to New Hampshire. Her baby had gone directly from the hospital to her new family.

"When I got home, it was dreadful," Lisette recalls. "I felt so guilty. Every time I saw someone I knew my face would get red."

Less than a month later, Ethan asked if she would like to move to New York with him, and she had no reservations. She packed her bags and took off.

Her parents were shocked. "There I was living in sin just after having had this illegitimate child," Lisette observes. "My poor mother." The following year, she found herself pregnant again.

In New York, Lisette held a low-paying though reliable job, but Ethan was involved in the theater and worked only sporadically. "I supported him," she says. "That was always the pattern of our marriage."

When her pregnancy forced her to give up her job, they returned to New Hampshire to live with his parents. Lisette got a job typing mailing labels at home and Ethan didn't do much of anything.

"We got married on my mother's birthday," Lisettte recalls, "which was also my daughter's birthday. Each year on our anniversary, it was a dreadful day. I would just weep and weep."

Karl was born several months after the marriage and Lisette was momentarily content. She had not wanted a baby yet, but she felt he would begin to fill the void left by the baby she had surrendered. Even so, it was a difficult time.

Ethan's parents didn't seem to mind that he lived off them. His father had been a musician in his younger days, but after having five children, he worked as a tool designer. His mother—"beautiful, absolutely stunning," Lisette remembers—had been a radio announcer, "but after five children and no time to care for herself, all she did was hit the bottle."

Nine months after Karl was born, Lisette, Ethan, and the baby moved in with Lisette's parents, where the expectations were quite different from what had been the case at Ethan's parents' house. Lisette's mother did not tolerate anyone who sat around wasting time, living like a parasite, and she made that clear. Within a few weeks, Ethan had a job as newspaper photographer. "That's what my mother does to you," Lisette explains. They eventually moved to their own home in another town, but Ethan continued to go through long periods of unemployment. He also began to carry on with other women.

During the years that followed, Lisette basically put the secret behind her. She never spoke of her daughter and tried to focus on Karl. Every once in a while, however, she would become depressed and despondent, frightened for the child she had given up.

As the wave of newspaper stories documenting child abuse swelled in the early 1980s, she found herself the victim of recurrent nightmares centering on her daughter. "Is she being sexually abused? Beaten? It was just a horrifying feeling to me to think that my child could be one of these kids and that I had no control over it because I had given up my rights. I'd left myself no avenue to find out if she were with good people."

At times she flirted with the idea of trying to get her daughter's files opened, but then she would remind herself, "You made a decision and you have to live with it." She also realized that as frightened as she was for her daughter, she was also terrified for herself. "Did I really want to know what had happened to her? Was that going to make it even more painful?"

Wounded by Ethan's tendency toward infidelity and tired of working to support his indolence, Lisette filed for divorce. "When they've been married a long time," she comments, "women often worry about being alone and self-supporting. But I had always been the one who supported us anyway, so that was no challenge." Lisette had worked in different settings, including a law office and a real estate agency. She eventually developed a successful career in public relations.

Ravaged by feelings of fury and rejection, Ethan decided to fight for Karl's custody even though he had not worked for a long period of time and had no way of supporting a child. Nine months after she filed, just two weeks before their court date, he got a job.

Karl was thirteen, and according to New Hampshire law a child that age could choose which parent he wished to live with so long as there were no overt extenuating circumstances. "Karl had to take the stand and make his choice in front of me, in front of his father," Lisette recalls, trembling as she continues. "The judge said, 'Who do you want to live with?' and Karl said, 'I want to live with my father.' The judge said, 'Why?' and Karl said, 'Because my father needs me.' The judge said, 'What about your mother?' And he said, 'She can take care of herself.' "

So bitter were the court proceedings that Ethan and Lisette have barely spoken since. At one point shortly after the divorce, Lisette recalls, Karl was having drug and drinking problems. "I called Ethan and said, 'We've got to communicate about our son if nothing else. He's having this problem.' His response to me was, 'He only does it when he's with you.' Like it was all my fault."

Lisette continued to see Karl through the years, but their relationship was a shambles.

Ethan, in the meantime, has carved out a career for himself as a radio journalist. He also makes documentaries and hosts a regional public television show, all of which give him considerable local recognition. Lisette runs her own public relations firm and earns a respectable living. Despite the fact that they have built independent lives, their rare exchanges continue to be vitriolic, and Lisette's relationship with Karl has suffered as a result.

"There were times when I never wanted to see my son again," Lisette admits. When Karl graduated from high school, however, Lisette decided to make a big effort and took him on a trip to Europe.

"I thought, 'We'll be completely away,' she said. " 'We'll work this out.' What a mistake! It was terrible. He didn't like what I said. He didn't like how I looked. He didn't like anything about me. And I wasn't very tolerant of him either. It was a terrible three weeks."

It is only now, with Karl in his mid-twenties, that Lisette has finally begun to enjoy a comfortable relationship with him, yet she feels it is still far from honest. "I think that he's growing up and developing a different perspective. He's separating who we are as people from our roles as his mother and daddy." If she says anything derogatory about Ethan, however, Karl immediately rises to his father's defense. She wants to clear her own conscience by telling him all the reasons she had for initiating the divorce and all the reasons why she was never able to restructure a friendly relationship with his father afterward, but she feels stunned by her son's defensiveness.

In addition, she says, "Karl has used both Ethan and me to his advantage and we both knew it. But what do you do? He manipulated me outrageously and I let him do it. I knew he was doing it and I let him, because I'm not sure he knew what he was doing. He's not malicious or vicious or any of those things. He's just a kid," she concludes, "a very young twenty-seven."

About two years ago Lisette was at work in her office when she got a call from a social worker asking if her name was Lisette Maclin (her maiden name) and if she had had a child at the Florence Hastings Crittendon Home. The caller identified herself as a social worker and explained that her daughter was looking for her. Did Lisette want to be found? Stunned, Lisette said that she would call back.

"My whole body was shaking," she remembers. "All these things went through my mind. Of course I want to meet her. I don't know if I do. What's the situation? Why does she want to find me now? Does she hate me?"

She set up an appointment with the social worker to explore her questions and came back feeling elated. "The things I was finding out were wonderful," she says, "and I was feeling enormous relief. After twenty-six years, just knowing she was okay. . . . She had Air Force parents, who treated her well. They adopted another girl two years later, so she had a sister. She lived in various places and she had everything she needed, everything that I couldn't have given her. It was like a load was taken off my shoulders. I felt younger, lighter. I felt released. But nobody knew about her yet, so she was still my secret."

Lisette asked the social worker to find out some other things about her daughter: the color of her eyes, how much she weighed, her height, the color of her hair. She later discovered that Olivia had asked for exactly the same information about her. About two weeks after the initial phone call, Lisette asked the social worker to tell Olivia her mother had been located, and to write to her, not to call. While she insists that the reason she asked her not to call was because she wanted to talk to her the first time in person, it is difficult not to speculate that Lisette feared her daughter would reject and resent her. She kept secret from Olivia the fact that it took two weeks from the time the social worker first contacted her to the time she agreed to meet her daughter.

"I didn't think that she would understand my hesitation or what I had to work through before I could be open to a reunion," she says, in her own defense. They exchanged several letters and photographs, and Olivia, who lives in Texas, announced that she would like to come to the Northeast to meet Lisette. Lisette agreed. Then she panicked.

"Telling Karl, " she says, "turned out to be the hardest part. He was in his last year of college at the time. I went to tell him after Thanksgiving as he was studying for finals. I didn't tell him because I didn't know how he was going to react and I didn't want to blow his exams. When exams were over, I went back but he was recording in his studio— he's a classical guitarist—and he was all intense, so I didn't tell him again." Karl spent Christmas with his father, as he did every year. With less than two weeks before Olivia's arrival, Lisette knew she was running out of time. "So I went to his house with all these presents," she says, "and he opened them and I said, 'Well, I have another present for you. It's something I have to tell you.' " After several false starts, with Karl now pacing the floor, she told him about Olivia.

"She was obviously terrified that I would hate her or something," says Karl, picking up the story, "but it didn't really surprise me at all to find I had a sister. Strange things happen to me all the time. This was just another one. I thought it was really neat. I was an only child until I was twenty-four. I wanted to know what she looked like. I wanted to know where she was, if I was going to meet her. I was sort of curious about who her father was, but Mom seemed a little reticent to talk much about that."

"My family keeps secrets all the time," Karl continues. Then he adds facetiously, "I guess that's why I'm so normal!" He goes on to observe that "getting any information at all is so darn rare that you don't push. If you do, they just clam up so there's no point to it." When asked what sort of information was kept from him, Karl answers "Well, knowing what time we're having dinner would have helped." Although the comment is sloughed off lightly, it seems to resonate with a longing for order and predictability.

Yet Karl is quick to defend his mother in her choice not to tell him of Olivia. "The way I figure it," he says, "she had a life before she had me. Things that happened after I was born, they affect me more directly, but before I was born, that's really up to her. That's her life. It's not part of my life. I mean, I'm curious, but if she doesn't want to tell me, that's alright."

It is not unusual in his family, he continues, for people to live double lives. "My father had two apartments at one point while he was still married to my mother," he offers, "and my uncle Alan, one of my father's brothers, was a screaming homosexual who was married for years."

In Karl's family it appears that it is not always safe for people simply to be who they are, to accept themselves at face value. They manufacture secrets as part of their concerted effort to maintain some control over the image of themselves they present to the world.

For Karl, growing up in an unpredictable world where both commitment and clear limits were illusive qualities, the fallout is insecurity, self-doubt, and a certain cynicism about how the world works. The paradox here is that on the surface, his paternal grandmother's house was a tolerant place where anything was okay.

At Lucy Arland's house, drinking was a way of life and work and discipline were considered far less important than marching to one's own drummer. "That was where you went if you were fourteen and needed a case of beer," Karl explains. "You asked my grandmother to get it and she'd say, 'What do you want? Give me the money.' Other kids were told to stay away from that place." Asked if it was difficult to be a grandchild in that situation, Karl answers with a cynical laugh. "Well, it seemed pretty normal to me."

The theme of normalcy runs throughout his commentary. At one point he recalls a paper on parent/child relationships he was assigned in an expository writing class. "I looked at my family and thought, am I supposed to find a norm here? This isn't going to make sense to anybody."

Karl is utterly convinced that his parents married only to atone for their previous mistakes. His conception gave both Ethan and Lisette the opportunity to do the right thing, which neither had done before. His maternal grandmother, he claims, never really believed that his parents were married until they got divorced. For Karl, his parents married but they never committed themselves fully, either to each other or to him.

When Karl was fourteen, his uncle discovered that he had a girlfriend. The uncle told him to be "real careful because look what happened to your father," implying that Ethan had fathered a child before Karl. "I sort of believed him," Karl muses, "sort of. But I never asked my father. There didn't really seem like there was a reason for me to."

Much later, when Karl told his father about Olivia's appearance, Ethan intimated that like Lisette, he too might be the parent of another child. According to Karl, he said, "You shouldn't be surprised if there's another knock at the door someday," and that the person doing the knocking would be a woman about ten years older than he.

Karl also recalls that when he first became involved with girls, his mother always asked, with great interest, "How old is she? What's her birthday?" In retrospect, he thinks her questions make sense. "I guess one of her great fears was that I would find myself attracted to my half sister, because she had no idea where this person was."

After exchanging letters with Lisette for several months, Olivia came to visit. She's been back several times since. When asked what the first meeting was like, Karl describes, with great animation, a videotape Lisette and Olivia made commemorating the event.

"It shows their first day together—my mother and Olivia. My mother was living in a tiny town at the time, three hundred people. There's a little post office and outside it there's a blackboard and every time there's a baby born in town, they write it on the board. So there's this videotape with Mother sitting on the steps of the post office and Olivia all wrapped up in this sort of swaddling cloth. On the blackboard it says, 'Baby girl Olivia, height 5'4", weight 127 lbs.' And then in large capital letters it says, 'OUCH.' It's the most bizarre thing."

In describing his own feelings for Olivia, Karl cannot say that he feels any deep bond with her based on blood ties. Then he counters, "But what's having a sister supposed to feel like anyway?" The more Karl talks about Olivia, the more frustrated he grows. He finds her materialistic, self-centered, and shallow.

Karl feels that Olivia's reappearance has affected his relationship with their mother. "My mother was so afraid that I would think she was some sort of slut," he explains, "but I don't see her that way at all. I never did. And I guess I still don't understand why she would think I'd see her that way." He thinks that their relationship is more positive now that Lisette recognizes that he doesn't judge her. "I think that was a revelation to her, that the way I see her was about 180 degrees from the way she thought I saw her."

For Lisette, who formed and perpetuated the secret, Olivia's appearance has also uncorked a barrage of feelings. Relieved to find that her nightmares were only dreams and that Olivia had not been abused as she had feared, she was able to lay aside some portion of guilt and uncertainty.

Accepted by Karl, whose rejection she feared, she has been able to relinquish some of her fears of estrangement from her son.

Ironically, in disclosing one secret, Lisette unearthed another. "When I went to tell my family about it, my brothers and sisters, I found out that they already knew. For twenty-six years they knew this about me but they never said a word. I felt deeply deceived."

4

When Illness Is Invisible

A S children, most of us perceive our parents as strong and powerful. We sense that they are responsible for our survival, that they are our ticket to safety in a complex world. That's why our sense of security can be so severely rattled when one of our parents becomes seriously ill.

As we grow up, we often equate physical infirmity with weakness, robust health with strength. So when a parent gets sick, our sense of weak and strong can become distorted. Suddenly our protector is transformed into someone who is fragile and who himself needs to be cared for and protected. Who then will care for us? While we may worry about our parent and the pain he or she is experiencing, as children what we worry about most is ourselves and the implications of our parent's illness for our own happiness and wellbeing.

When an adult is gravely ill and a child hears whispers behind closed doors but never gets any clear information, the child often feels excluded, diminished, and frightened.

The imagination soars and scenes of imminent death may flourish. Some children are plagued by visions of outrageous, uncontrollable pain, while others are seized with overwhelming feelings of guilt. Without accurate information, children resort to their own resources to fill in the vacuum.

Often, though not always, when the illness is a physical one there is concrete evidence of the extent to which our parent is incapacitated. Even when parents are reticent to share information about their condition, when the illness is physical we at least have an amorphous understanding that something is not right, and that the changes in our household are somehow attributable to the fact that a parent's body is not working properly. When someone is physically sick, relatives and neighbors often provide comfort and assistance. Their offers of help and their expressions of concern serve to remind us that the reason our lives are in upheaval is because our mother or father is sick.

When the incapacity takes the form of mental illness, however, the concrete evidence may be absent. The friends and family may keep their distance, unsure whether or not to intrude. When a parent suffers severe mental illness, children need even more help in understanding what is going on.

Bizarre behavior may be much more confusing than casts and intravenous apparatus. When secrets form around mental illness, they build barriers between members of a family just when they need each other most. Often constructed to protect the image of the family, the fences are propped up by shame, fear, and ignorance. Because we fear what others may think, we try to conceal our difficulties from them. In doing so, we deprive ourselves of the support and nourishment that we so vitally need.

What happens when family members conceal mental illness, either by shielding the sick person from the greater community or by refusing to acknowledge the illness even within the family? Are we afraid we will be ostracized, tormented, or scowled upon if we let out the truth? Whom are we protecting by keeping it secret? The more forthright our parents are in describing their disease and the way it affects them and the family, and the more opportunities they provide for us to ask questions and to voice our fears and feelings, the better we are able to deal with the difficulties that ensue.

Natalie and Claudia

Natalie Rosenberg-Zellman was the youngest child in a comfortable middle-class family with a sister and brother, two and three years older than she. The son of immigrants, her father was an American success story who put himself through law school, became a bank commissioner, then a state representative, and finally a judge. Mrs. Rosenberg stayed at home, a fulltime housewife and mother, but before she married she had run her family's sewing machine factory, while her brothers went off to war.

Now in her early forties, Natalie was nine when her mother committed suicide in 1957. Mrs. Rosenberg was first hospitalized about two months after the family moved into a new house in a new neigborhood. Natalie was in the fourth grade. "When my mother was first hospitalized, my father told me it was because she fainted and that there was something wrong with her heart," Natalie reminisces. Then she adds, "That was a lie."

While Natalie was told that her mother was in a hospital, she never knew it was a mental institution even though her father took her there to visit. For her it didn't seem all that different from the hospital where she had once visited her grandmother after she had had a heart attack. The visits always took place in a pleasant living room or out in the garden. "I never saw her in her room," Natalie observes. "I never really had any idea where we were going. We visited this pretty country place and we'd sit around and talk. She was always knitting. I remember her crying too. And she'd hug me." Yet Natalie never questioned her father's explanation that her mother was suffering from a heart condition.

Prolonged periods of hospitalization became hallmarks of the last two years of Mrs. Rosenberg's life. While Natalie thought her mother was being treated for a coronary ailment, in truth she was receiving electroshock therapy treatments for acute depression. During this time, Mrs. Rosenberg sometimes returned home for weekend visits. It was during one of those visits that she took her own life by closing herself up in the garage, running the car, and inhaling carbon monoxide.

The police came to the house and Natalie remembers hearing one of them say, "She's gone." She also recalls hearing her father express his guilt, telling the policeman that maybe he could have prevented it, and the officer saying, "You really couldn't have. There are knives, there are lots of other ways. . . ."

When Natalie's mother died, her father telephoned an aunt who immediately came and fetched her. Natalie went to stay with her relatives for over a week, separated from her father, brother, and sister and from the mourning activities at home. Although she knew that her mother was dead and that she had killed herself, she felt like she was walking in a dream.

"They took me to a carnival in the rain," she says, "and I remember thinking, 'But my mother just died.'" When she returned home, she remembers turning on the televison and hearing her father say, "You can't watch television." When she asked him why, he said, "Well, we're in mourning." This was confusing since otherwise she had been excluded from the mourning formalities.

"My father wouldn't let me go to the funeral," she recalls. "He wouldn't let me participate in the shiva, where everybody comes to the house. That was very bad for me. I used to have dreams that my mother wasn't really dead, that she was coming back. Maybe if I had gone to the funeral I wouldn't have had those dreams. I wasn't a part of it." Yet she is quick to defend her father. "I think my father was brought up in the school of thought that said if you don't talk about it, you don't need to understand it. Maybe he was sheltering me."

Natalie is convinced that her father would have kept the cause of her mother's death secret from her, as he had kept secret the nature of her illness, if he had had the opportunity.

"In Jewish religion," she explains, "there's a very bad stigma associated with suicide. Taking your own life, you're not even supposed to be buried in the same cemetery as other people. So I felt that shame, and I wouldn't talk about what happened to anyone. I was so afraid that my classmates would find out."

Life changed drastically after Mrs. Rosenberg's death. Although she had not been a regular presence in the household for nearly two years, she had influenced the mood there.

"My father adored her," Natalie explains, "and after she died he would cry a lot. He never got over it." Nor did he ever really talk about it, choosing instead to relegate his memories of his wife, her illness, and suicide to a hidden corner of his mind.

Shortly before his death at eighty-two, Natalie's father talked to her about her mother's death for the first time. "He said, 'You know, your mother committed suicide,' and I said, 'Yes.' Then he said, 'I don't want to talk about that.' "

Another time Natalie's father told her that before they married, her mother had been engaged to another man and that he had committed suicide. "Then he asked me, 'Do you think I could have done anything? Do you think I could have talked about it and saved her life?' And I said, 'No, I think you did all you could.' "

Now the mother of three children herself, one of them a nine-year-old daughter, Natalie shakes her head as she tries to imagine herself at that age, wondering why she never asked her father about her mother's illness and death.

"I think I knew that there were certain areas you just didn't get into," she muses. "I knew very clearly that this was one of those areas. I think my father once said, 'I can't talk about it. It's too painful.' He didn't think this was an area that I should get into and I trusted him. I think that I accepted his protection."

Natalie, who is now a successful business executive, always felt strongly about having a career of her own. This was partly because her father served as a strong role model, and partly because she didn't want to be a housewife like her mother. And while she always felt confident of her ability to prove herself as a professional, she is quick to acknowledge that she suffered real doubts about her capacity to be a good mother. When she tries to remember what her family was like before her mother went away, she says,

"I think about her being home and I think about her not liking to go out very much, in contrast to my father, who had tons of friends and was always going out, to wakes, to banquets, and visiting clients." She believes her mother had been ill for a long time before she was hospitalized and that, in a sense, even when she was with her children she wasn't completely there.

"I think my experience with my mother deprived me of my belief in my own ability to be a mother," she says. "I didn't have an instinctive feel for mothering because my mother hadn't been able to feel that for me."

Natalie's insecurities were reinforced by her husband, Nathan, who believed that children should be brought up by professional nannies. When their first child was born, a nanny was hired and Natalie found herself pushed out of her baby's life. She feels this created problems in her relationship with her oldest child which persist into the present. When asked why she let that happen, she says, "I didn't have confidence in myself. I didn't know that I could be a mother. And my husband later admitted that he didn't think I could be a good mother either."

It wasn't until six years and two children later that Natalie mustered the courage to stand up to her husband and dispense with the caretaker. Because the true nature of her mother's condition was concealed, Natalie was never given the opportunity to think about her mother's detachment as a symptom of her illness. Instead, she interpreted it as a trait or deficiency which was handed on to her.

While Natalie's family concealed information from her as a child, her husband's family leaned toward the opposite extreme. Nathan grew up in a family beset with financial problems. His father was an entrepreneur who started one business after another in a cycle of failures. His parents went into great detail in explaining their tribulations to him.

"By the time Nathan was an adolescent," Natalie comments, "it was all put on his shoulders. He'd come home from school and he'd be told that this didn't work out and that didn't work out and it was just too much." As a result, Nathan tells his own children very little of his business life.

While Natalie agrees that the children shouldn't be burdened with the details, she does feel they should be kept abreast of what is happening in general terms. She thinks her kids need some explanation of why their father acts the way he does when, for example, they go shopping and he loses his temper.

"When a recent business deal of Nathan's fell apart," she explains, "I did tell the kids about it as a way of letting them know why he was so preoccupied."

But while she is painstaking in keeping her children informed about the realities of the present, Natalie is more reticent to share details of the past with them. According to Natalie, her fifteen-year-old, Ruth, is "very fragile. I'd be concerned about telling her. She tends to be very inward, almost narcissistic. I'm afraid if I told her she'd say, 'Oh, it's hereditary.' " Yet Natalie's experience has convinced her of the wisdom of being straightforward and truthful.

Five years ago, when Natalie's youngest daughter was four, she was diagnosed as having neurofibromatosis, a serious progressive disease. "I had a hard time talking about it at first," Natalie remembers. While she told her older children that "Emily has neurofibromatosis and we're going to have to take her to a lot of doctors," she didn't really tell them what that meant. When her oldest child became very tense and insisted that the disease was genetic and that she would get it too, Natalie realized how vital it was that she share more information with her kids. "I had to sit down then and explain everything that was going on," she says. "And when Emily developed cirrhosis of the liver, I explained about that. I really laid it out for them and they appreciated that.

"Now when Emily asks me questions—she has a friend with neurofibromatosis who just lost an eye and she said, 'Will I be like that?'—I'll say, 'Well, it could happen but let's hope it doesn't.' I always give her total information. Kids like Emily, they can develop tumors on their nerve endings. She could get cancer. She could become deformed. She knows all that. I think knowledge is very important."

In an effort to stabilize their own relationship and develop some common ground in how they manage their children, Natalie and Nathan see a marriage counselor and their children know that they do.

"A lot of the issues that we discuss have to do with how we relate to the kids," Natalie explains, "so it's important for them to know what we're working on. We don't talk about the specific content of what we discuss, but we tell them that we're working on some problems that we hope will make our family life better."

For Natalie, the family secret was mental illness. For her older sister Claudia, the hidden truth was suicide. Not that she didn't know that her mother had taken her own life, but it was a subject so forbidden that, as she says, "We didn't talk about it for more than twenty years."

The first time she ever heard the event mentioned in the presence of her siblings was when her father died in 1980 and the rabbi asked how her mother had died. Her brother

Jake told him, but that was all. The subject was quickly sequestered away in the privacy of each child's memory.

Claudia is incredulous to hear Natalie say that she did not know that their mother was mentally ill.

"I certainly knew she was depressed," she says. "I sensed she was vulnerable. I remember her talking about how life wasn't worth living. She'd talk about how she wasn't worth anything and I'd try to tell her nice things so that she would feel better." She knew too that when her mother was hospitalized it was because of emotional problems. She even knew that her mother was getting shock treatments.

As Claudia's oldest daughter turned twelve, the age that she herself had been when her mother died, Claudia became aware of an increasing amount of tension between the two of them.

"I'm basically very devoted to my children," she says, "but I found myself getting angry at stupid things, and I eventually realized it had nothing to do with the kids." Claudia entered therapy and began to work very hard to recall details of her mother's death, details that she had always been aware of but that she had never verbalized before.

"I never had anyone to talk with about this," she explains, adding that her father would start to weep if anyone even mentioned her mother's name. "So the kids had to protect him," she continues, "and to protect him we had to be sure not to cry. He was the only parent we had left and if you've had a parent die, you worry because you've got all your eggs in one basket. If our father got depressed and took *his* life, then what would we do?"

As the oldest child, Claudia began to assume aspects of her mother's role in the family. "Natalie was my father's baby and Jake was the angry son, and I was the parentified child," she says, "so obviously my brother and sister were going to resent me." Yet the more Claudia speaks, the clearer her own resentment becomes. Deprived of her adolescence, she sought approval by trying to fill her mother's shoes, smoldering inside all the while, her grief transformed into anger over having no opportunity to be a child, to express her feelings, and to seek the comfort she so desperately needed.

Claudia channeled all her energy into being competent. Yet she could not do enough. "I was my father's companion," she says. "And I paid a very high price for my relationship with him. We had a housekeeper but I did a lot of the cooking. We would have a seder and I would do everything, except that Natalie would make the chopped liver. And then everyone would say, 'What great chopped liver!' I had done everything else, absolutely everything. But she was the baby. That's the way it went."

Although Claudia was never expressly told that the conditions of her mother's death were a secret, she learned by example. The party line, perpetuated by her father and adult relatives, was that her mother had died of a heart attack. Claudia knew this was not true but she didn't know who else knew.

"When you have a secret," she muses, "you don't know what other people know or don't know about what's going on. For me, that meant I never really knew if I was reading things right. I mean, did people know or didn't they? For my brother, well he always felt like people were talking behind his back."

Looking back, Claudia thinks her life would have been very different had she been encouraged to talk openly and truthfully about what had happened. "I've always held myself back in a certain way," she explains. "I always felt this anger in me, and now I realize it was really grief that was never expressed. Any child who's faced with a trauma like this, there's a reaction of shock. What happened to me was that this shock just got perpetuated because I couldn't talk about it. So I built a wall around it and that's when the steel doors slammed shut."

The first step in healing the damage caused by the long-held secret was to confront her feelings of anger—anger at having lost her childhood, at having lost her mother, at having to remain silent and isolated in her pain. The second step was to break the secret open to her daughter, which Claudia chose to do with the help of her therapist. "It was a big deal for me to tell Rebecca," she says. "She burst into tears. Whenever someone in my family is missing, maybe just a little late, I go bananas. Well, when my mother died, I woke up and couldn't find her and I went looking for her in the woods."

For Rebecca, who resented what she saw as her mother's overprotectiveness, the revelation brought relief. "My daughter thought I didn't trust her," Claudia continues, "but suddenly she understood why I panic whenever she's late or I can't find her. It was like an incredible burden was lifted from her. Telling her the secret, that my mother had committed suicide and what that did to me, cemented our relationship."

When Claudia told her daughter the secret, she asked her not to share it with the two younger kids. "Rebecca accepted what I asked," Claudia reflects, "but it put tremendous pressure on her relationship with her nine-year-old sister, who saw us getting closer and closer while she felt more and more left out." Realizing that it was a mistake to withhold the information, Claudia told her second child the secret. Soon after, she told her six-year-old son. "It was a wonderful relief," she sighs, "to have them all know."

Raised in the Northeast, Claudia has made her home in Georgia for the past twenty years. In that time she's become acculturated to regional mores. She says, "It's like there are two levels of communication in Southern society. There's the polite level, and there's the buried level. A lot of times people here hide things. They want everything to look nice on the surface."

Claudia adapted well to cultivating a pretty surface demeanor, until she dealt with the residue of her own family troubles. Once she had acknowledged and integrated her secret into the rest of her life, she found she was no longer able to remain soft-spoken on issues that provoke tough, painful feelings. Since surrendering her secret, she's become an ardent activist, an outspoken advocate for children, and has gained a degree of notoriety for her opposition to corporal punishment in schools, which is still legal in Georgia.

By coming to terms with her own experience, she has gotten in touch with what it feels like to be a child in an unfair situation. "I have empathy for children who are helpless," she explains, "and I speak out when I think something is wrong. Before I was sort of wishy-washy about things, but now I know there are certain issues that I really care about. I'm convinced that the whole world would be a lot better off if life were better for children. That's the way I make meaning out of my suffering."

Anna

Anna Lieber's father committed suicide just before his forty-fifth birthday, when Anna was nineteen.

"It was his second suicide attempt in two weeks," she says quietly, "although my mother wouldn't acknowledge the first one."

It was Anna who started making telephone calls looking for her father when he failed to return home after work one evening. When the police arrived later that night, it was Anna who answered the door. She was the first to hear the news. "They had found him," she recalls. "He had driven to a park out of town and killed himself with a rifle."

Anna's thirteen-year-old sister, Sherry, and her ten-year-old brother, Adrian, were asleep. "I was extremely distraught," Anna remembers. "When my mother told me she wanted to keep how my father died a secret, even from the other kids, I agreed with that. I think now that that was a big mistake. It cut me off from my brother and sister and there have been a lot of problems ever since."

In the days following Stephen Lieber's death, Anna's mother, Martha, fell apart and Anna assumed the role of parent. She bought a cemetery plot and selected a casket and, at her mother's insistence, arranged to have a wake.

"Looking back," she says, "my behavior was very bizarre. My role was to comfort everyone who came in crying. In retrospect, it wasn't healthy for me to do that."

From the start, Anna experienced an intense, almost physical need to talk about her father and what he had done, but the only one she could speak to was her mother and her mother did not want to hear. Martha forbade her daughter to tell anyone the secret, not even her aunts and uncles.

Stephen Lieber came from a large South Carolina family and all ten of his siblings had stayed in that part of the country. "My father had been out to visit his family just before this happened," Anna explains, "and they knew something was wrong but they didn't know what."

Anna's mother told them that Stephen died of a massive stroke. "But it was not a well-kept secret," Anna comments, "because my mother would sort of change the story depending upon whom she talked to. She would change the location where it happened. She told my brother and sister that he had had a stroke in the middle of the night and that the ambulance had taken him away. Several years later we went down south for a family reunion and she told the relatives that he had died in our car. My brother got hysterical. He said, 'Wait a minute. These are two different stories.' " Even then, Martha didn't tell him the truth.

Anna was living away from home by that time and, after that, whenever her brother would call her he'd say, "When you talk to me about our father, you don't look me straight in the eye and I know that you're lying. I want to know the truth." Then Anna would call her mother and beseech Martha to let her set the record straight, but her mother would say, "Absolutely not, not under any circumstances."

"It was always very important to my mother that everything be perfect," Anna explains. "We grew up with the expectation that there wouldn't be any problems. They just weren't allowed. We were the perfect 'Leave It to Beaver' type family. If we had problems, our mother withdrew from us and we just felt very isolated and lonely."

As Anna looks back on her childhood, she realizes that her father was always depressed and very separated from the family. Because he had to leave school and go to work after his own father died, Stephen never had a college education, a fact which smarted more and more as he climbed the ranks in his business. Eventually vice president of a successful brokerage company, he provided his family with a conventional upper middle-class lifestyle, but he was never at peace with himself. When he was transferred to the home office and surrounded with Ivy League graduates, his sense of self began to deteriorate rapidly.

Anna was born right after World War II and Stephen and Martha entered into a compact stating that she would handle the baby and the home, and that he would be free to establish himself professionally. Even Martha admits that Stephen interpreted the agreement in the extreme.

"When he came home from the office and I was little, I had to be put away, out of sight," Anna relates. By the time her sister Sherry was born six years later, Stephen was a bit more ready to be a parent, although only on his terms.

"My sister had access to our father that I didn't have," Anna explains. "She knew that she could sit next to him as long as she followed the rule, which was not to say anything. I could never do that. I always wanted verbal contact. Sherry says what she got wasn't nearly enough—it was just a little more than I got—but from my perspective it was a lot."

As the oldest child by far, Anna tried to endear herself to her father by taking on chores more commonly associated with sons. She mowed the lawn, waxed the car, painted the shutters, and generally did anything she could to please her father, but he remained indifferent.

"There were great silences in my house," Anna observes, but their extremes were as nothing compared to what Stephen experienced as a child. His own father used to line up all the kids in the parlor and order them to watch while he knocked their mother to the floor and kicked her.

"When my father married my mother," Anna explains, "he told her that he had a terrible temper and that he never wanted her to push him because he didn't know what would happen if he lost control. So there would be days when my parents didn't talk to each other. There would be incredible, stressful silences in the house. So things were not comfortable. It was a very neat, very orderly house. When Dad was at home, we couldn't have any playmates over. Plus, we had to fit into his schedule."

Stephen also exhibited compulsive behavior that left its mark on his children. The atmosphere at home was extremely rigid. He expected dinner to be on the table five minutes after he walked into the house, and it absolutely had to follow a prescribed pattern: chicken on Monday, steak on Tuesday, and so forth. "It was a very difficult environment to grow up in," Anna concludes.

Three and a half years after her father's death, Anna married and her mother remarried, both in the same month. Anna's stepfather brought three children to his marriage. It was then that the pattern of secrets began to intensify.

Anna's brother Adrian was only thirteen at the time. He was so disturbed by his father's death and the other changes in his life that he began to skip school, spending whole days roaming in the swamplands. Martha would get a call from the school, but instead of recognizing that Adrian needed help, she'd lie to her husband and she'd lie to the school authorities, covering up for her son.

According to Anna, there was intense competition between her mother and stepfather as to who was the better parent, which meant that instead of reaching out to a child in need, Martha covered Adrian's tracks so that her husband wouldn't notice he'd drifted astray.

By this point Martha's kids felt themselves squarely pitted against their stepfather's kids. With Anna married and Sherry away at school, Adrian bore the brunt of the hostility, and he says now that he felt abandoned.

"My stepfather is a nice person," Anna observes, "but he doesn't connect emotionally. He wanted to be part of a big family—he thought that would be wonderful—but he didn't understand about adjustments. He just expected us to fall into place. But the strain was enormous."

Anna's mother couldn't admit that Adrian needed help because that would mean that her family was blemished. Even later, when he was a teenager and in danger of dropping out of high school, Martha manipulated the truth in order to preserve the image she presented to outsiders. She and Adrian would go to counseling sessions together, and she would tell the counselor the story she thought he wanted to hear. "She would paint a picture that had nothing to do with reality," Anna says.

"Adrian wasn't going to graduate from high school," Anna explains, "but because I'm involved in special education, I was able to pull a few strings so he got his high school diploma. But he never felt good about it because he knows he didn't really earn it. From the time he graduated, he's never been able to do anything consistently. His pattern has been one of starting things and then not being able to finish. He would start so many projects and then be completely overwhelmed. From time to time, I would sit down with my mother and say, 'Look, he needs help. Let's tell him the secret and see what's going on.' But she would always order me not to. And I've always been a good little girl who did as I was told."

Yet Anna remained convinced that the secret had some connection to her brother's problems, simply because Adrian would not let the subject rest. He continued to ask about it throughout the years, as though he knew innately that something important had been withheld from him.

Anna's husband, Mal, eventually gave Adrian a job. One day he had to reprimand him because he wasn't doing what he was supposed to be doing. Adrian broke down in tears and told Mal that he wasn't able to sleep or concentrate. He also described other symptoms of depression. Adrian mentioned too that he didn't know how his father had died, that he had been too little to remember him very well but that he had a feeling there were shadows surrounding his death.

"As it turns out," Anna explains, "he imagined things far worse than suicide. He thought that maybe our father was an axe murderer or some sort of really evil person, and that quality had been passed down through his genes. But what was really causing his depression was that he thought he was doomed to have a massive stroke in his forties and die, so why should he pursue a career? Why should he get married and have children?"

When Mal related Adrian's outpouring to her, Anna told herself that no matter what her mother thought, Adrian had to know the truth. Mal said Adrian could continue to work for him on the condition that he see a psychiatrist. Once he was hooked up with a doctor, Anna called the therapist and told him the story and he agreed that Adrian needed to know. "So I went to his next session and told him there. He hated me as we walked out of the office," Anna says. "Why had I betrayed him? Why didn't I value my relationship with him strongly enough to override our mother?"

Adrian's rage toward Anna lasted only about a week. It was replaced by a flood of relief, although he was still upset and angry at his mother. He insisted that they needed to tell Sherry, their sister, and that they needed to tell their father's relatives. He wanted to fly out to South Carolina immediately, and then continue on to New Orleans where their sister lived with her husband. "I felt we should tell my sister first, do one thing at a time," Anna says.

As it happened, Anna ended up telling Sherry the story on the phone. Sherry reacted by pursuing all the details she could get regarding her father's death. She wrote to the coroners. She called the police and got their record. "It was very graphic," Anna says quietly. "I had just pictured it in a different way. I never had a need to know all the details.

"I was the last one to see him alive," she continues. "He left in the morning and drove to a state park and apparently spent the whole day walking around the car. He had worn a path, so obviously he was in a lot of turmoil, a lot of pain. It was in the evening that he killed himself. He placed the gun in his mouth and pulled the trigger. The report detailed what part of his head was left and what part was all over the car. I found it very disturbing."

Again, Anna was the target of fury. Sherry, like Adrian, was enraged that she had put her relationship with her mother ahead of her relationship with them. She expressed her anger by insisting that Anna do things for her, such as calling the president of the company their father had worked for. Anxious to appease, Anna did as she was asked. "It turned out he knew what had happened," she says. "There were all sorts of liability issues though and when I called, he was not at all pleased to hear from me."

Sherry persisted in her need to know why her father took his own life. Martha, who was furious at Anna for breaking eighteen years of silence, insists that it was just an odd event, that Stephen was fine, and that she has no idea why he committed suicide, a position which she maintains even today. "She still paints a rosy picture," Anna says, shaking her head, "where everything was wonderful. We had no problems. It was just one of those odd events in life you can't explain."

Martha's reaction, her insistence that nothing was wrong, further infuriated Sherry. When Anna realized how disturbed her sister was by the deception and by Martha's denial, she decided that she needed to share with Sherry all the information she had regarding their family, whether or not directly related to their father's death. As she started to pull back the curtains, Anna also began to realize the extent to which her mother had drawn her into collusion over the years and, consequently, the enormous distance she had placed between her and her siblings.

"Mother had confided all sorts of things in me: that she had had a marriage annulled before she married my father, that my father was four years younger than she, all kinds of things about Adrian. But I couldn't go anywhere with any of it. And any feelings I had about any of it had to be blocked. The only person I could talk to was her, but she didn't want to hear things that would make her sad. So I was put in the position of having to say that I was fine, that I was handling it, when the fact was I wasn't doing very well at all."

In the years following her father's death, Anna and her mother became what Anna now views as abnormally close. "Because we shared the suicide, she was the only person I could confide in and talk to."

Throughout her life, Anna comments, "Mother has been sort of the hub of the wheel. She had everybody separated and she acted as the go-between," a role Martha continues to play and one which Anna now views as manipulative and offensive. The more Anna asserts herself, most particularly by breaking open the secret, the more she becomes the focus of her mother's anger.

When Anna and her siblings confronted their mother with their interpretation of how they were raised, Martha became incensed and defensive. "She says that the way she grew up was much worse than the way we did," Anna explains, "and that she has no apologies to make. She says she's suffered far more than we have and that she doesn't want to hear what we have to say. And she says that I'm being dramatic, focusing on all the negatives and not recognizing the positive things, like that Daddy was a wonderful father. But in fact he was not, not to any of us. He rejected me, and I wanted so much to have a close relationship with him. I kept trying to connect with him but he would be cruel, often making a joke at my expense. He didn't like to be talked to, and here I am, working with children with communication disabilities—that can't be an accident.

"I think we were all very afraid of Mother," Anna continues. "She was like a banker. She had all the love and to get that love, we all had to do what she wanted, which was to smile and say everything was okay, and if we had problems, not to tell her because they made her feel sad.

"I broke the secret just this past year," she continues. What is particularly tragic to her is that her father's twin brother recently committed suicide exactly the way Stephen did, by putting a gun in his mouth. The brother had never known how Stephen died, and Anna believes that if he had known, he might have gotten some help for himself.

Anna's aunt, sister to the uncle who died and to Anna's father, wrote to Martha at that time and asked how Stephen had died, if he had taken his own life. Anna's mother didn't respond to the letter.

"She wasn't even going to tell the rest of us how our uncle died until my brother started turning suicidal and I decided that he had to know everything, about our father too," Anna explains. Up until this time, the only people who knew how Stephen Lieber died, other than the police and his employer, were Anna and her husband, her mother and her second husband, and her mother's minister.

While Sherry and Adrian understand why their mother initially kept their father's suicide secret, what they cannot forgive is her persistance in keeping the secret for fourteen years—until Anna took it out of her hands.

"My brother is very, very angry," Anna comments. "He says I gave him back his life when I told him the secret, which is wonderful. He had never been able to separate from my mother because she made him feel entirely responsible for her wellbeing, her health, and her life, which is a feeling Sherry and I have experienced too, a sense of being totally responsible for her happiness. Adrian thought that if he left her, she would die. She really gave him that feeling."

Adrian was twenty-four and still living at home when Anna told him the secret. Within two months he moved out, got his own apartment, and started to piece his life together.

Right after her father died, Anna recalls, "I felt that it was absolutely inevitable that I would commit suicide." Although Anna knew the truth, her inability to share it and to sort through the feelings she experienced after her father's death sentenced her to the same sort of sense of doom that pervaded Adrian's life.

For Sherry, the realities of her upbringing combined with the deception to impart a legacy of resignation. "Of the three of us," Anna explains, "my sister is the one who tends to feel hopeless about situations, whatever they are, rather than feeling that you can do something to change them."

As Anna, Sherry, and Adrian continued to compare their growing-up years, they discovered that they all experienced their mother in the same way—manipulative and isolating, the strict arbiter who decided what could and could not be expressed. The difference was in how they reacted. While Adrian and Sherry to some extent acted out their troubles, Anna just kept on smiling.

"My mother needed me to be the model child," she says, "the oldest child who's happy and who achieves, for whom everything is fine. And the price for not playing that role would have been that she would ignore me and not talk to me. My father already didn't talk to me, so in order to survive I thought I needed to play that role. And I continued to play it after my father died. If I displeased her, she would stop talking and I remember feeling that I would do anything, just anything, to get her to talk to me."

For Adrian, learning the truth has given him a new lease on life. "For him," she says, "the demons of the past are gone. He's in control. He doesn't have to stay connected with Mother. He can lead his own life." He continues to feel enormous anger toward his mother, and hardly ever sees her. And while that may be healthy for him, it has had an unfortunate impact on Anna. As her mother and step-

father become increasingly bitter about Adrian's with-
drawal, they focus their anger on Anna. "It's my fault," she
says simply, "because I told him what happened."

Anna is convinced that her life would have been very
different if she had been able to talk about her father's
death from the start. Not only would it have allowed her to
connect with her brother and sister, relationships which
instead grew increasingly superficial, but it would have
enabled her to make better, healthier choices in her own
personal relationships.

"The continuing torture for me," she says, "is that the
person I married is just like my father. And I didn't have
any glimmer of recognition before we married. It was like,
I can marry my father and this time do it right. My mother
had allowed me to assume a lot of guilt. I was implicated in
his wanting to kill himself. I had felt sort of responsible for
my father's suicide because there were a whole lot of emotional things going on between us. So this time, I would do
it right."

But what Anna discovered is that she cannot remake the
past through her husband. She cannot fix him to atone for
the loneliness and rejection she experienced in her relationship with her father. Instead, she finds herself on the brink
of divorce, tormented at times by suicidal feelings herself.

Like her father, her husband holds his children at arm's
length. He is critical and rejecting. And like her mother,
Anna realizes that she wanted her own children to be perfect, to be happy. While she thought she was raising her
kids differently from the way her mother raised her, she
realizes now that she funneled pressure onto her oldest son.
"My younger son has severe disabilities," she says, "and my
daughter has mild learning disabilities. So my relationship

with the two younger children was always empathetic, sort of like with my clients."

Her older son, Allen, however, began to feel increasingly isolated in the family. One day when they were alone together in the car he said, "Mommy, I think being in heaven would be better than being alive." Anna stopped the car and asked him, "Honey, have you ever thought about committing suicide?" Allen answered, "Yes." They went home and Anna called her minister. He met with Allen and the next evening he took him to see a psychiatrist.

"My husband thought I was overreacting and that Allen was just being dramatic," Anna notes. When the minister returned late that evening, he explained that the doctor thought Allen should be hospitalized because he had thought out specific ways to kill himself. "He had said he was feeling unsafe and that he would be very relieved to be in the hospital." Anna's husband objected. He didn't want to spend the money. Anna insisted that Allen go.

"He did go and now he's thriving," she says. "Now that I've told him and the other children about my father, he feels that he's the one who blew the whistle and said, 'This isn't good enough. I'm not happy.' " Anna told Allen the secret while he was in the hospital and she told him too that he was free to talk about it even though his grandmother, Martha, might not like it. She also explained to him that she had not yet broken the secret to his brother and sister but that she hoped to do that soon. At the time, Allen was angry at his siblings and was delighted to collude with his mother in keeping the secret from them.

As therapeutic as the hospitalization was for Allen, unfortunately it hammered another wedge between his parents. The stress eventually took its toll on Anna and she too was hospitalized with suicidal feelings. Her husband's reaction to her breakdown further exacerbated their problems. He told the kids that their mother was away on vacation.

"I was wild," Anna says. "I felt my kids needed to know what was happening with me and the staff at the hospital felt they needed to know." Eventually Mal brought the children to the hospital, where Anna answered their questions. I told them I was there because I needed to get help because of how I was feeling."

Shortly after she left the hospital, the whole family made a Memorial Day trip to the cemetery where Anna's father and her maternal grandmother are buried. Anna's younger kids still didn't know the secret. They had never really considered that their mother had a father other than the stepfather that they knew and thought of as their grandfather. They started asking questions and she started answering them. Mal got angrier and angrier, but Anna didn't stop. "When I finished the story," she says, smiling, "my daughter said, 'No wonder you've been sad. No wonder Nana's strange. That's why you were in the hospital. That's why you needed to talk about things.' Then she said, 'Thank you for telling us the truth.' "

Anna's story is still far from complete. She remains a victim, choked by the web her mother spun when she first drew her into complicity. She is, however, no longer a prisoner in that web.

"So many things have happened since I broke the secret," she says. "Allen and I are getting help and I think that's where my sense of hope comes from. Things are very tense now, not good at all, at home, and the kids keep asking me if we're going to get a divorce and I tell them I don't know. I'd love to tell them 'Of course not,' but I can't. They'd love to hear a different answer but at least they know I'll tell them the truth. At least they know when I say I don't know, I really mean that. And they know too that they can talk about what's going on at home, that they don't have to keep it a secret."

Carolyn

Carolyn Mondello, in her early thirties, has a twin sister, another sister one year younger, and a brother thirteen years her junior. She was brought up in an attractive suburban neighborhood with a mother who stayed at home with her children and a father who worked as a technician for a large company. On the surface, hers was an average, unsurprising American middle-class family. Just beneath the surface, circumstances revealed quite a different picture.

"My father is mentally ill. That was the big secret in our house," Carolyn says, coming straight to the point. She adds that her mother Doreen is chronically depressed and agoraphobic, meaning that she fears leaving her house. For Carolyn's mother, secrecy made its mark on her marriage, right from the start.

As far back as Carolyn can remember, her mother told the kids that she and Martin, their father, had known each other for six months before they married. When Carolyn was in her twenties, her mother finally told her that the story wasn't true. She and Martin had only known each other six weeks and, Carolyn explains, "The marriage was a kind of set-up deal between my mother's aunt and my father's mother. I think my mother was sort of embarrassed about whom she married and she wanted to make it seem like it wasn't such a rush job, to make it more proper."

Doreen and Martin had a lavish wedding, which his parents paid for. "They were into appearances," Carolyn states succinctly. The idea, she says, was that her mother, a lovely, nurturing person who had a great need to be needed, would take care of bright, volatile Martin.

Martin's family was financially well off and had a large house, and Carolyn is convinced that her mother's need for security was part of her motivation in marrying him. "She sacrificed her life for security," Carolyn says. "It was very important to her that we would be well-supported economically."

When she was in her twenties, Carolyn and her sisters hosted an eightieth birthday party for their maternal grandmother. Listening to the stories the old people told, Carolyn realized for the first time just how poor her mother had been growing up. She knew that her mother's father had died when she was very young but, she says, "I never knew that my mother and grandmother had lived in a boarding house before my mother was married. That really shocked me."

Doreen was twenty-four and Martin was twenty-six when they married. Piecing together stories from her mother, Carolyn is certain her father's problems were evident early in the relationship. Her mother once told her that while she and Martin were engaged, they were playing Monopoly one night and the game wasn't going well for Martin so he grabbed the board and threw it across the room.

"She was shocked," Carolyn observes, "but he was very handsome and brooding. I think she saw him as sort of a

Heathcliff figure and that she was very attracted to him sensually. I think too that she believed that the love of a good woman would transform him." Three months after the wedding, Doreen was pregnant.

Recounting the chronology, Carolyn breaks her story abruptly and says, "There's a secret my father still doesn't know. My grandmother gave birth to him when she was thirty-seven and after that she had two abortions on the kitchen table. She wasn't crazy about having kids. She told that to my mother but not to my father. I think she knew he couldn't handle that. And I think the deal was that Doreen's job was going to be to take care of Martin. She told this to my mother and my mother told me after my grandmother died."

Another secret that Doreen kept from Martin is that she dosed him with tranquilizers for many years without his knowledge. Doreen's mother "had a family doctor who knew Martin was really crazy," Carolyn explains, "so she got a prescription for something like Elavil and my mother fed him this stuff for a long time, but then the doctor died so the source dried up."

While Doreen was pregnant with what turned out to be Carolyn and her twin sister Alice, Martin beat her up. She fled to her mother who said, "You're married, you've made this commitment. Go back to your husband where you belong."

When the babies were born a few months later, the situation worsened. "Not only were we twins," Carolyn says, "but we were very premature. Alice weighed about four pounds and I only weighed a little over three. I was in the hospital for six weeks but Alice went home sooner. And right from the beginning, my father was enraged at us for taking away his 'mother.'" Not only did both babies need lots of care, but three months later Doreen was pregnant with Erin, who was born a few days after the twins' first birthday. "So," Carolyn concludes, "Martin never got the attention he needed."

As Carolyn tells her story, there are times when she cries and times when she laughs. Throughout, she periodically affirms her love and loyalty to her mother, and yet she does not sugarcoat the realities of what it was like growing up in her family. She seems to have remarkable access to her feelings as she pours forth unequivocal observations.

"I've never heard my father say my name, never," she says. "Ever since I was little, I've always been referred to as 'the jerk.' The only time he ever touched me, except for the times he slapped me, was when he shook my hand when I graduated from college."

In describing her father's illness she says, "He's paranoid. He has delusions. He has auditory hallucinations. He has schizoid breaks. He's sadistic. He doesn't have any friends. He's a very, very sick man."

In trying to recreate the fabric of her childhood, Carolyn says, "Whenever we'd go out in public, it was pretty horrible because he was like an explosive and you didn't know whether he'd go off or not. We'd be in a department store or a restaurant and my mother would say something and he'd kick her, his face all scrunched up. Sometimes there were fights in parking lots. There was a lot of shame involved."

She remembers an incident when the family was together in the car. Her father was driving and Carolyn was sitting in the backseat, chewing gum. "He caught my eye in the rearview mirror, turned around and slammed me in the face and said, 'Don't you ever dare stick out your tongue at me again!' "

When asked if her father has ever been institutionalized for his problems, she answers, "No, my mother is his institution." In fact, his illness has never been professionally diagnosed or treated. When Doreen once suggested that he see a psychiatrist, she ended up with two black eyes.

Carolyn and her siblings obediently colluded with their mother to protect the image of their family. As a child, Carolyn recalls the strain of always lying about why her parents never attended any events at school. "We'd make excuses because our mother told us to. For years and years we hid the secret of my father. He's crazy. That's the secret. Mother would say, 'Don't talk to people about your father,' and Alice and Erin and Matthew and I kept the secret from the whole world, because we loved our mother and we wanted to make her happy and to protect her from what other people might think."

Looking back, Carolyn sighs as she thinks about the continual strain involved in keeping up the facade. "I'm tired of secrets, really tired," she says. "It takes a lot of energy to keep them, to make up reasons why your father can't be there, why you can't be in a carpool, why this and why that. It's exhausting. And I think a lot of the joy that should be part of being a kid was not there for us, which is very sad. We were not very spontaneous children.

"I would hide whenever my father came into a room," she continues, "but that didn't happen too much because the way the household ran, well, my mother basically choreographed it so that we kids would be in one place and my father would be upstairs in his room and we'd never be in the same room together. He would have his meals on a tray in his room. It was so horrible growing up in my house that it's extremely difficult to convey how awful it was."

Carolyn says flatly, "I thought it was that way for most people. We lived in a suburban neighborhood, tract housing. In the family on one side of us, the father committed suicide. In the family on the other side, the father ran off with another woman. There was a neighbor up the street who was just as strange and nasty as my father. So that was kind of the way I grew up, assuming that men are weird, that the woman's role is to protect and hide and keep secrets so that these dysfunctional men can kind of make their way in the world. If the women didn't do this, then all hell would break loose."

Despite his illness, Martin has always held a job and supported his family and as long as Carolyn can remember, he's worked the swing shift, 3 p.m. to 11 p.m., which minimizes contact with coworkers and with his family at home. The schedule enabled Carolyn and her siblings to have playmates over after school, but visitors were never allowed in the house when Martin was home. "We couldn't have any friends over when he was in the house," she says, "because you never knew what might happen."

Martin continues today to work as a technician, repairing missile parts for a large corporation where he's been employed for thirty years. The people he works with are much younger than he. Some of them are almost fresh out of high school.

"Apparently these kids he works with now are very needy and socially inept themselves," Carolyn observes, "and they've picked up on my father's paranoia and made him their target. They harass him, stick nails under his car and things like that. He works in a sort of a cubicle and the most horrible thing that happened was once when he went to pull his chair back and they had tied a string to the chair and to a bucket they'd placed on a shelf above his desk. The bucket was full of urine, which spilled on his head." Because Martin's behavior is bizarre and because he elicits the worst in his coworkers, the company would like to can him, but they don't because he's a member of the union and the union is very strong. "He's hanging on by a thread, waiting for early retirement."

For Carolyn, making excuses and keeping secrets didn't stop when she left home. She lived with her husband, Sam, for several years before they were married and her father never knew that. Her mother knew, and she wanted Carolyn to keep it a secret from both her father and brother. "My brother was a senior in high school then," Carolyn says, "and she thought it would be terrible for him to know. But I told him. I said, 'Matthew, Mom wants me to keep a secret but I'm going to tell it to you like it is.' My mother is really into secrets, within the family. I think she does it because she's afraid everything will fall apart, but the way I see it, she's been living in hell. I guess it's a hell that she knows."

When Carolyn and Sam got married, Martin did not come to the wedding. The excuse Carolyn and her family made for him was that he wasn't happy because his daughter, a Jew, was marrying a Catholic. "That's one of the reasons, but the real reason is that he's crazy," Carolyn comments, adding that she has not seen him in five years even though she lives less than an hour from him and sees her mother frequently.

Matthew was only six when Carolyn left for college. His relationship with his father is different from that of his sisters in that Martin does talk to him. For years Doreen felt it was such a big step to have her husband even speak to one of the children that she constantly cautioned Carolyn against telling her brother about their father. She feared that the slightest interference would poison whatever existed between father and son. When Carolyn confronted her, saying, "Don't you think Matthew's going to figure out that Dad's really crazy?" Doreen responded by saying, "Let him do it in his own time." Carolyn obeyed. "I'm a good daughter," she says, "and I love my mother. I could tell she was trying to keep the lid on a boiling pot and I didn't want to get in the way."

When her brother became a high school senior, however, Carolyn took him on a weekend of college visits. They were sitting together in a campus coffee shop when he looked directly at her and said, "Do you think Dad's weird?" That was the start of the first conversation the two had ever had about their father.

"He was seventeen and I was thirty," Carolyn recalls. "We talked for a few hours. He told me that his earliest memories were of hiding under the bed so Dad wouldn't see him. And I said that I used to do that too. He said, 'You're kidding!' " Matthew was very agitated. He felt that he had been isolated, left to fend for himself while his older sisters sought solace in distancing themselves from the family. He was angry at Carolyn for leaving him to cope with his own fears and suspicions, never offering comfort or confirmation of what he suspected. He resented her for leaving him to question his own sanity rather than clearly pinning the craziness on their father. "Finally," Carolyn continues, "I told him that the reason I never said anything was that Doreen had said not to."

While Doreen rigorously insisted that Carolyn not speak about Martin, she indirectly encouraged her kids to count on each other to compensate. "My sisters and brother and I are all very, very close and I think that's because our mother always gave us the message that even though our father was crazy, we had each other."

In a sense, each member of the family knew the secret, and setting it aside simply meant not covering up anymore, not presenting a facade to the rest of the world. At some point while she was in college, Carolyn went to her mother and said, "Doreen, it's too much. We can't keep it a secret anymore. Our father is crazy, our life is crazy, and that's it. We're not going to hide it anymore because it's too hard for us." Doreen reacted by saying, "Alright, if that's what you want." Yet to this day, she will not herself talk openly about Martin with her children or anyone else.

"It's important for my sisters and brother and me just to say, 'He's crazy!' " Carolyn explains. "It diffuses so much of the tension. And because of the way we grew up, tension diffusion is very important to us.

"But if I really stopped and thought about my mother's life," she says, "it would destroy me. So it's like, this is the way it is. I'm her friend. That's all I can do."

The secret may be broken for the kids, but for Doreen the ruse continues. Martin is still crazy. He still does not get any help, and Doreen continues to serve as his link to the world, his protector, and in a sense, his accomplice.

Marta

When Marta Orlando's husband returns home from a trip to visit his parents, she plans to tell him she wants a divorce. She is tired of hauling him out of barrooms, tired of not being able to count on him. With three small daughters to care for—a seven year old and ten-year-old twins, one of whom is retarded and legally blind—she knows that the road ahead will be a hard one. She also knows that she cannot live with an alcoholic anymore, even though Sal works steadily and is well liked by their friends and by Marta's family.

When she tells her children about the impending divorce, Marta will tell them the truth. Her own childhood was riddled with secrets, and she does not want to repeat the pattern with her kids.

Brought up in a Catholic working class family in the 1960s, Marta has five brothers and sisters. She calls herself the youngest of the older kids, who were all born a year or two apart. After Marta's birth, five years passed before the other two siblings—the younger kids—were born. Speaking of her two older brothers, her older sister, and herself, she says, "We were four really close, fun kids. We sort of brought one another up and played together and fought a lot, but we really liked each other."

Of all the children, Marta says she was the closest to their father. She says too that she always felt a strong need for his companionship and affection. A self-described tomboy, Marta collected baseball cards passionately and loved to go to Yankees games with her father. He would take her to the games alone and she doesn't remember his doing that with any of the other kids.

The Orlando kids were brought up Catholic. They went to church every Sunday. For Marta, Catholicism evoked strong feelings of guilt. Going to church made her feel confused and embarrassed, largely because her parents sent the kids but didn't attend themselves. "The nuns would say things like 'Where's your Bible?' and I would think we must be terrible because we didn't have a Bible, and because my parents weren't there."

"We were an adorable family," Marta continues. "Wonderful children, nice house. All very sweet. We weren't rich at all but we looked solid, steady. The only thing is, something else was going on." It wasn't until much later that Marta realized that the something else was alcoholism.

Many children who grow up with alcoholism become expert at deception. It is as though they are actors on a stage, visible to the public and determined to hide the chaos taking place in the wings. They struggle to protect the image of their family, because they intuit early on that other families are frightened by families like theirs, that other parents may caution their children to stay away from them. Many feel they would be betraying their parents if they let outsiders know about their problems. Embarrassment and humiliation are familiar companions, as these children channel their energy into concealing their parents' behavior. They do not understand that alcoholism is an illness. Like Marta, sometimes they do not even know that the problems in their family are caused by alcoholism.

Children who grow up with alcoholic parents often sacrifice their childhood as they struggle to assume responsibilities that their parents ignore or are unable to manage. They grow up far too quickly. Not only do they suffer from their parents' inability to provide them with the physical and emotional support children need to grow strong and healthy, but they are called upon to confer exactly that kind of nurturance on the very adults who should be giving it to them. As a result, many grow up feeling wounded, resentful, and empty.

Too many disappointments, too little care, and too much fighting erode their capacity to trust, making it difficult for them to forge solid, mutually gratifying relationships as adults. They find that their suffering does not end when they grow old enough to leave their parents' home and strike out on their own. Rather, it seems to go on and on, until they are provoked to get the help they need in order to face, instead of deny, the painful burden they carry from having grown up with alcoholism.

By the time she was about ten, the same age as her own twins are now, Marta became deeply aware that there were cracks in the family facade. Her parents began to bicker at neighborhood parties as her father's drinking increased. She remembers hearing about one social gathering where her father got into a fistfight with a neighbor. She also remembers very vividly the night the police came to the house to take him into custody for getting drunk and causing a disturbance.

"My brothers had to restrain my father from going after the police," Marta says, "and I saw all that." The police took him away to jail and, Marta continues, "The next day my father came home really down and out. We didn't know what to say to each other. Everyone was just a bundle of nerves." Yet Marta's parents never talked to their children about the incident.

When Marta was about eleven, she thinks her parents may have tried a separation. Like many other important events that happened in her family, the separation had no clear beginning or end. She was told that her father would be going away for awhile, to work somewhere else. He came back after a couple of months, but then he left again, a week here, a week there. She never understood why or where he went, and neither of her parents ever offered any explanation. Indeed, she understood that she wasn't supposed to ask, but simply to accept.

When Marta was thirteen, her parents divorced and her father left for good. But no one told her or her brothers and sisters.

Just as her father's excessive drinking and the problems it caused were never discussed, neither was the divorce and her father's subsequent disappearance. Marta, however, can clearly remember the night her father left for the last time.

Her older brothers and sister had all gone out for the evening and the two younger kids were asleep. She remembers that her father came home drunk and her parents had a big fight. "I just kind of crept into my room and kept my ears opened," she says. She remembers the screaming and she remembers hearing her mother yell, "You get out of here and if you ever come back again I'll kill you." Her father left and he didn't come back.

The next day, one of her siblings wondered where Dad was and then a day or so later, she recalls her sister asking, "Where's Dad?" Marta told her that there had been a big fight and that she didn't think their father was coming home anymore. As the weeks passed, she realized she was right.

"It was very secretive," she says. "There was an abrupt break, where all of a sudden my father was gone and there was a divorce. It was like that was the end of my father's life as a person. He just became a real bad drunk. My father disappeared and never gave my mother a dime."

Marta remembers that her mother went on welfare right away. Her mother's energy went into trying to hang on to the house and she offered virtually no emotional support to the older kids. Marta remembers one time when her mother told her please to stay away from the house after school because a social worker would be coming over. Later she realized that her mother was trying to protect her from the stigma that she associated with welfare, alcoholism, and divorce.

Marta says that her mother reacted to the divorce by rapidly making a lot of changes and by distancing herself from the family. "My mother went back to school," she says, "and she got a job, and she started dating. All very quickly. She sort of left us. She had gotten married at sixteen and had all these babies and had to take care of herself the best she could. So her message to us, the four older kids, was 'You kids are grown up enough now to take care of yourselves.' " At thirteen, Marta understood the message and responded to it by becoming fiercely independent, but she suffered inside.

As a ceramics artist who often works with high school students, Marta now has a lot of contact with teenagers. She knows what a difficult period adolescence is and how much support kids need to get through it. It makes her sad to remember how little nurturing and guidance she got during that part of her life. "Basically," she says, "I started working when I was fifteen. I pretty much supported myself. But nobody ever knew what was going on in my life. I quit school, but no one cared. I felt real abandonment, especially considering my father's relationship with me when I was little. It was neglect.

"At thirteen," Marta continues, "I had a real good opinion of myself. I knew I had strengths." But after the divorce, she says, "I withdrew forever. I just got sadder and sadder. I didn't feel good about my family or myself. I felt really bad that my father was in the condition he was in. I tried to protect him. I had friends but I wasn't really close to them. Most of them never knew about my home life. I don't remember ever being consciously dishonest, but I know I put up a wall to keep people from asking questions. And I didn't take friends home."

The younger two kids were six and eight when the divorce took place. Whatever mothering Marta's mother was able to do, she centered on these two. The older kids also worried about them. Their father had visitation rights but he hardly ever exercised them. Marta remembers how her little brother Davey would wait and wait by the door for their father to come see him. But when he did occasionally make plans to visit, often he didn't show up.

Even now, twenty-one years after her parents' divorce, Marta says that her father still pulls stuff like that with her little brother. Watching the way her father treats Davey and still stinging from memories of how he abandoned her, Marta has quit all contact with her father, who continues to drink heavily.

As Marta tells her story, she keeps returning to the intensity of the relationship she shared with her father as a young child. It is that very closeness, she thinks, that made the drinking, the divorce, and the subsequent abandonment so destructive to her. It is as though the closeness itself was a ruse, a half truth. As a result, she has difficulty trusting her own feelings and her perception of reality.

As a teenager she dated lots of guys, but as soon as one really seemed to care about her and treat her well, she'd break up with him. "When someone started getting serious with me," she says, "I'd feel like, 'What could you possibly see in me?' I just didn't think they'd like me anymore if they knew where I was coming from. I mean, no one cared about me at home. I didn't have much self-esteem, I guess."

Like many adult children of alcoholics, when she married, Marta found herself caught up in repeating the pattern of emotional neglect she knew too well from her childhood. "From the moment I came into this relationship," she says of her marriage to Sal, "I wasn't really getting any of my needs met. Basically, I think I chose someone who was going to neglect me and emotionally abandon me and not be there for me. It was familiar. That's why I felt so comfortable with him."

Sal was a year ahead of her in high school and she admired him and liked his friends. After he graduated, he became an accomplished mason and eventually started his own business. When they started living together, Marta was twenty. She was working and taking college courses, earning money and not making any demands on him. They spent most evenings with his friends, enjoying themselves. Then Marta got pregnant and they decided to get married.

Marta figured that when the baby was born, she would keep on working part-time and that there wouldn't really have to be too many changes. She was used to taking care of herself and she figured she could handle this without putting too many ripples in her relationship with Sal. But her plans went askew when she discovered she was carrying twins.

Cassie and Nora were born when Marta was only six months pregnant. Both were expected to die. "They were in the hospital for three months," she says, "and Cassie was handicapped. So all of a sudden I went from being very independent and sociable to being very dependent and intensely involved with these two babies. I basically handled all the problems and Sal basically went to work and showed up at home only when he wanted to. He gave me money so I could raise the kids but he resented my being so dependent on him." Sal also resented the fact that Marta could no longer hang out with him and his friends.

Marta enjoyed taking care of the babies, despite the difficulties. "I wanted this to work more than anything," she says, "and I tried and tried, but Sal kept retreating." Sal worked from six in the morning until seven at night, six or seven days a week. When she urged him to be involved with her and the kids, he'd say, "I'm working all the time. How can you ask me for help?" When Sandy was born three years later, the situation deteriorated even more.

It was around that time that Sal started going to bars after work and not coming home until he got thrown out or the place closed. Sometimes he'd stay out overnight. Desperate to take back some control of her life, Marta set down a hard and fast rule. If Sal wasn't home by 8:00 PM to say goodnight to the kids, she'd lock the doors and he could find somewhere else to stay. Several times when he didn't show up, she bundled up her three little kids and drove around to the bars until she found him.

"I'd take the kids in and tell him to get out of there, in front of all those men," she says. "Sometimes he'd make us wait. He'd say, 'I'll come when I finish my beer.'"

She followed through on her threat several times, locking him out for the night, and then Sal started coming home. "I tried to put the choice to him," she says. "You either drink and stay out all night and don't come home to your family, or you just get yourself on home at a reasonable hour. That was the only power I had, and it worked.

It's kept him in line for the last three years, but we don't have a marriage."

After a bad incident, Sal always felt horrible. He knew that Marta would be furious and he tried to appease her anger. "We call this 'the house that guilt built,' Marta laughs softly, gesturing to the piles of lumber near her deck. "Every good spate of work on this house happened after my husband had done something bad. After he went on a binge, he'd bring in carpenters to make me happy."

Despite his drinking, Sal continued to work steadily and eventually started his own construction company. Marta's understanding was that by incorporating his own business, he could protect his family's personal assets, including their house. With all her energy funneled into raising the three kids, Marta left the business totally to Sal, who gave her money for household bills. Last year she was shocked to discover that the company was bankrupt and that there were $45,000 in liens on her home. Sal had kept their financial troubles secret from her.

Marta says that in the meantime, she too had been keeping a secret. She had led Sal's family to believe that she and Sal were getting along well. She never told them about Sal's drinking. But after she discovered the bankruptcy and the liens, she did tell his parents, about both the drinking and their financial problems. Sal was furious. He felt betrayed and humiliated. For Marta, telling his parents was part of her effort to stop hiding their troubles, to bring them out in the open so they can be resolved. For her, resolution means divorce. Sal is vehemently opposed, but she is determined to go forward with her plan.

Marta knows that she needs to tell her kids. She doesn't want to spring a divorce on them the way her parents sprang it on her. "I'd like my children to know what happened to me," she says, "to understand that when their dad is nice to me, it's usually after he's done something that hurts my feelings."

Marta goes on to describe nights when she's kept dinner waiting for Sal and he hasn't shown up, or when he's told her he'd be home at a certain hour so they could do something as a family, and then has gone drinking instead. "I told him one night," she says, "that when you do that to me, I feel the same way I did when my father took off. I have the same feeling inside. It's a real anxious, sad feeling, an abandoned feeling. He looked like he was taking in what I was saying, but then a few days later he did it again. He went drinking and didn't show up when he said he would."

As she marshals the courage she needs to end her marriage, Marta experiences conflicting feelings. "I'm scared to death," she says, "but I'm also probably the happiest I've been in years." She knows that she will not have an easy time. Raising a severely handicapped child is a difficult task for the most stable of families; doing it alone with two other children, limited financial resources, and the challenge of negotiating with an alcoholic ex-husband sounds almost impossible, but Marta is optimistic.

Her sense of hope is rooted in the enormous relief she feels now that she is confronting the pain of her childhood and taking steps to provide herself and her children with a healthier life. She knows now that she is not to blame for the pain she feels. For Marta, the pretending is almost over. She has joined an adult child of alcoholics support group and continues to see a therapist. She has told Sal's family she plans to get a divorce, her own family knows, and all of their friends know. "But," she says, "Sal still won't accept it and the kids don't know exactly what's going on." Her next step, she says, is to get her children into counseling.

"I know I can't deal with all the problems ahead by myself," Marta explains. She adds that she is very angry at her parents for not getting her and her brothers and sisters the professional help she thinks they needed. "I want someone to help me figure out what my kids can understand," she says. Marta wants her children to be able to express and respect their own feelings, and she wants to help them understand that their father is an alcoholic and what that means for them.

"I don't want to keep any secrets from my kids," Marta says with conviction. "I don't know what's going to hurt them and how to help them. But I do know I can't do it alone. So I'm going to get help with that. We really need to make sure that all the damage that has been done, to them and to me, comes out."

5

Some Parents Are Gay

J UST a couple of decades ago, the expression "coming out" was reserved for debutantes, young women about to "come out" to society. For most of us now, saying that someone has just come out means that person has purposefully revealed that he or she is gay. Simple enough on the surface, coming out means being public about one's sexual orientation. It means making social adjustments and giving up old pretenses in favor of the desire for acceptance of oneself as is. Coming out is a statement of truth, of reality. It is often a tortuous, painful step, entwined with cracking open secrets and laying to rest longstanding misconceptions.

For some, the step is the culmination of years of living a double life accompanied by merciless self-examination. For others, it happens by default; the attempted cover-up just doesn't work anymore. However it happens, when a parent reveals that he or she is gay, the effects reverberate. Coming out can open the door to pain and alienation, but it can also provide a passageway through that pain, a means of navigating through the muck and finding relief and acceptance.

Lisa

Fresh out of the Women's Corps in the early 1950s, Lisa Corning met her husband, Adam, at a dance at a veteran's college in upstate New York in the early 1950s. It was, she says, "love at first sight."

Adam had just gotten out of the Navy and for two months they were nearly inseparable. They spoke of marriage. Then, suddenly, Adam disappeared from campus without a word.

A week later, when Adam returned, Lisa was in the infirmary with a bad case of the flu. She asked him where he had been. She also asked him if they could get married.

With another patient in a bed just a few feet away, there wasn't much privacy. Adam told her that he had gone to New York City to see a psychiatrist and he passed her a note. The note said, "I am a homosexual." Lisa looked up at him and said, "What's that?"

Twenty-three years old, she had grown up in a small town in New Jersey. "My parents weren't educated," she says, "and we never mentioned things like that."

When Lisa got out of the infirmary, Adam suggested she talk to one of their psychology teachers, who was also gay. "He told me Adam was gay and what that was," she recalls. "I said, 'Does that mean we can't get married?' He said, 'No. Go ahead and try it for a few months and if it doesn't work out you can always get it annulled.' Then he said, 'Lisa, Adam is the worst homosexual I've ever known.' In other words, he didn't think Adam was practicing very much. He was trying to be reassuring." They were married a few weeks later in the college chapel.

Adam had never had a sexual encounter with a woman before Lisa and he was excited and gratified. He told Lisa that in marrying her, he had made up his mind that he could become heterosexual. He said that this was what he really wanted.

"He told me that he was miserable as a homosexual," Lisa remembers, "that all his friends were too, and that they'd give anything to be able to marry and have a family. And he said that most of his friends were very, very jealous that he'd found me." The first year sped by happily, the two of them very much in love, very popular as a couple, and very involved in campus life.

After graduation, Lisa and Adam took off for Paris to pursue an exotic Bohemian lifestyle. She studied French, he worked on an autobiographical book. They lived in Isadora Duncan's apartment with her brother and palled with Truman Capote. They also became involved in a ménage à trois.

"We both got involved with the same man," Lisa explains. "He was a great guy, an artist, and Adam and I are both still friends with him." Finally, they returned to the U.S. because, she says, "We were so poor we were eating radishes."

Back in New York, they set up housekeeping in a pleasant Greenwich Village apartment, where they stayed for three years. Lisa worked as a nurse and Adam got a teaching job. Lisa became pregnant and gave birth to Lydia, the first of three daughters. Although euphoric over the baby, Adam had started drinking regularly while they were in Paris and now drank even more.

"We'd have these wonderful parties," Lisa recalls, "and I was in complete denial about his drinking and about his homosexuality. We'd have months and months of bliss: holding hands, kissing, having sex." But there were problems too—not enough money, for one thing.

Through a stroke of good luck, they fell into a house-sitting situation in an affluent suburb north of New York. Adam got a job with the local school system and soon after, Emma was born.

Shortly after Emma's birth, while Lisa was commuting to her nursing job in the city every day, Adam became involved with one of his students.

"I'd come home from work," Lisa remembers, "and the two of them would be trying to take care of the baby and the older child. Adam was a wonderful father. He adored the kids, but when they cried, he couldn't take it. So I'd get there and this young guy would be pacing the floor with him. Adam swore there was nothing between them, but I was ashamed because I knew the neighbors thought this was a very odd relationship." There followed an onslaught of accusations, recriminations, and many tears, but no real changes.

Life continued, and two years later, Lisa found herself pregnant again. It was 1957 and abortion was illegal unless recommended by a physician. She went to New York to see a psychiatrist and tried to convince him that she needed to terminate her pregnancy.

"He refused to okay it, so I went ahead and had the child," she says.

Around this time, a book came out that dealt realistically with homosexuality. For Lisa, the book confirmed just how miserable she really was. In Lisa's words, "The author said that it was very convenient for a homosexual to get married because the wife acts as a shield and then he can have all the affairs that he wants and still have the respectability and protection of the home."

After Lisa's eyes were opened by the book, she'd find herself crying and crying, seemingly unable to stop. "The little kids would say, 'Mommy, why are you crying?' and I wouldn't be able to explain it to them." She adds that "from the beginning, I really led a double life because I could never tell any of my friends. I felt they would never understand." Now she felt cut off from her children as well.

By this time, Adam had found a position teaching psychology at a small college. A popular, dynamic faculty member, he also ran the theater program and a successful public speaking forum. Lisa worked as a school nurse and took college courses to get her bachelor's degree.

Commuting to class with three other women early each Saturday morning, Lisa and her friends talked a lot about their marriages and their children. "I always gave the impression that Adam and I had a lot of sex, which we hadn't had for a long time, and that everything was wonderful," Lisa says. "People envied us. We gave the impression of being the happiest couple around."

At home, when Adam wanted to cuddle Lisa cringed. "I would itch all over," she says. "I would walk the floor. He drank more and more and finally moved up into the attic with his bottles of sherry and whiskey."

"I always covered for Adam," she says, as she looks back on this time. "Nobody knew he was alcoholic, nobody knew he was gay except for the few gay people he went with."

Then things got worse. Sometimes Adam would go into New York, down to the waterfront, cruising. One time a group of thugs chased him to his car and beat on the windows. To protect his wife and children, he always left his identification at home so that if he got caught his name wouldn't get into the newspapers. "It got to the point," Lisa says, "that I hated his guts and I'd scream at him, 'I hate you, I hate you!' It was pretty horrible for my poor kids."

As the years passed, Adam's affairs became more frequent and his drinking more blatant. The household shuddered with late night fighting and screaming. Often Lisa's supervisor at work would express concern about her bloodshot eyes and drawn face. Lisa would lie and say that she had been up all night with a sick child.

One day she came home to find that Adam and one of his friends had been drinking and then had gone out in the garden and masturbated together. "I was sick about it," she says, worried about the neighbors, the children, about discovery. "But then we would go on for three or four months and nothing happened and everything seemed okay."

While the kids grew up in an explosive, hostile atmosphere, they never really knew what lay at the root of the dissension. They shared in polishing the image of their family for the outside world, but they did not share in the knowledge of the family secret. That changed when Lydia, the oldest, was sixteen. She needed some money and Adam told her to get it out of his wallet. When she did, a card fell out that said "Gay Liberation Front."

Lydia asked her father about the card and he told her that he was gay. Lydia went out to the garden where Lisa was sunbathing and asked her what that meant.

"I don't remember what I told her," Lisa says thoughtfully. "But much later, she told me that I told her too much." Lisa didn't ask Lydia not to tell the younger kids the secret, but she assumed she wouldn't. Emma, the middle daughter, was thirteen at the time. Of the three children, Emma is most like Adam, Lisa thinks. She has many of the control issues that are frequently found in children who grow up with an alcoholic parent. She needed to feel in charge, to feel that she could make order out of chaos, and one way she did that was to set limits with her father. Another way was to put herself in the role of her mother's caretaker.

In those days, Lisa and Adam separated frequently; it was the drinking, not the homosexuality, that led to the separations. "When Hemingway died," Lisa remembers, "Adam cried for three days. He identified with him. Then he'd drink and threaten to throw chairs out the window."

When Adam was living somewhere else, sometimes he'd call and ask if he could come home for supper. If Emma answered the phone, she might say, "Mommy, Daddy's drunk." And then they'd agree not to have him to supper.

"Emma had a lot of control," Lisa observes, "and then, she became my confidante. Not about his being gay. About his alcoholism. That was bad. I made a lot of mistakes."

Emma found out her father was gay when she stumbled on an article he had written called, pointedly enough, "I am a Homosexual." Adam's mother, a senior editor at *Reader's Digest,* had tried to get the story published.

"The magazine okayed it," Lisa remembers, "but then they decided the world wasn't ready for it."

When Emma found the article, she took it to Lydia for an explanation. They talked about it and then came to Lisa together.

"They were both fascinated by the whole idea that their father was homosexual," she says. "That's when we decided it was time for us to talk about it as a family, that we couldn't keep it from Hannah," who was then eleven.

"Hannah is very different from my other two kids," Lisa observes. "She's the engineer in the family. She's competent but she's not sensitive, and she hates the fact that the rest of us are all so emotional. She can't stand anyone having secrets from her and we knew she'd be furious if she found out accidently, so we all agreed to tell her." Adam sat down at the kitchen table with her and spread out the story. Hannah acted as if she weren't terribly interested, but years later Lisa discovered that she was really deeply disappointed with Adam as a father not because he was gay but because he couldn't fix things. He couldn't do anything mechanical. Her uncle, Adam's younger brother, could do all those things and she really wanted him for her father.

"After everybody knew," Lisa continues, "we were drawn together as a family. We were like a knot. Now we had this huge secret that we all shared in." Actually, she corrects herself, they had two secrets: Adam's homosexuality and his alcoholism.

The children understood how important it was to keep the secrets. First, there was the fear that Adam would lose his job. There was also a good possibility that Lisa would lose hers. She had by that time become the president of the board of health in a community of 170,000 people, and her name was constantly in the local newspaper.

Second, they feared that their personal safety would be at risk, that Adam might even be killed if the secret were to be disclosed. "At one point we lived around the corner from a man who'd murdered two homosexuals," Lisa recalls. It appeared the man, who was represented by a famous criminal lawyer, was on the verge of getting out of prison. Lydia, Emma, and Hannah went to school with the murderer's children. Adam and Lisa also feared that their children would be tormented if their father's homosexuality became public.

For the most part, the children kept silent. "Emma did tell one friend," Lisa remembers, "and the friend said something awful to her about her father being unnatural and abnormal. Emma dropped her as a friend, and the girl never seemed to understand why." After that, Emma became much more reserved and tentative about letting anyone know.

Lydia was absorbed in her own difficulties at that time, a maelstrom of crises that her mother attributes to the general tenor of the sixties. "She got involved in drugs," Lisa says. "She also had a couple of abortions. She was going through hell. She even tried to commit suicide a few times."

Lydia's own problems were so overwhelming that, from Lisa's perspective, she never really paid much attention to her father's situation. Hannah removed herself. "For her," Lisa explains, "it was like, that's Mommy's problem."

Adam and Lisa and the two younger kids traveled out West the next summer. It turned out to be a terrible trip, because Emma was feeling so angry and full of hatred toward Adam that she fought with him constantly and began eating compulsively. "She felt he was cheating on me, hurting me," Lisa says. Perhaps Emma also felt that in some way her father was also cheating her, by not being the father she had thought he was. Hannah, true to character, remained oblivious to the friction throughout the trip.

"What the secret did to our family," Lisa stresses, "was to make us feel very special, kind of proud that we were covering up for one another and that we could put on a good front, that we were so popular as a family and that nobody knew."

Then she pauses and adds quietly, "It was awful."

They continued to cover up, going about the task of getting by, until Adam was about fifty. At that time he told Lisa that he wanted one of his former students to move in with them as his lover. He was a young man in his early twenties whom Lisa knew well and whom she enjoyed.

"I said, 'I've been serving this guy tea and cookies and you've let me think of him as a family friend. How could you do this to me?' "

Adam explained that he and the young man had been carrying on an affair for about a year. They had tried to break up because of Lisa, but they couldn't do it.

Lisa felt as though she would be the laughing stock of the community. She was also terrified that Adam would leave if she didn't agree, that she wouldn't be able to support herself. In retrospect, she realizes how crazy that was. She was a trained nurse with a formidable resumé. She was the one who had scraped and borrowed and made excuses when they couldn't pay their bills.

"I covered for him for years because of the drinking," she says. "He had sixteen credit cards and he would run up these terrible debts. We had a Tiffany lamp and he sold it to get money for drinking. He sold his blood to blood banks to get money. He did everything, he was so desperate to drink. I felt as though I'd been through hell for him and now he tells me, he's got this guy and they want us all to share a home."

At an earlier point, when the kids were preadolescent and Adam was terribly sick from drinking, he got a friend to take him to Rockland State Hospital to have himself admitted for detoxification. When he got there, though, and found he'd have to sign a paper, he got scared. He'd lose his job. So he walked away. She mentions other incidents and then says, "Through all these horrible things we'd stuck it out and stuck it out, and then to have him suddenly confront me and say he wanted all three of us to live together. . . ."

Instead, they agreed to see a psychiatrist. First Lisa went alone a few times. She told the therapist that she wanted to separate, but that she found it very hard because Adam couldn't handle money, couldn't cook, couldn't take care of himself. She couldn't imagine how he'd get along without her. She also said that she was afraid to live alone. Adam joined her in a few sessions, but then Lisa made the decision to leave. She moved out with the two kids who were still at home, but she continued to clean Adam's apartment and they still did things as a family. The two men started living together. Lisa threw herself into her career.

"I worked terribly hard," she says, "because I needed something to fill my life. I did a lot of good stuff and I felt good about myself. Finally I got to the point where I could say, 'What am I going to do with my life? The two of them want to live together and I don't fit there. I've got to do something.' "

By this time, all three kids were living away from home. Lisa moved to Boston, got a graduate degree in psychology and counseling, took a job in the psychiatric unit of the Cambridge City Hospital, and made a new life for herself.

That was more than ten years ago, yet she and Adam have never divorced and she doubts they ever will. The children have developed their own lives but continue to be in touch with both parents, although the family is now spread out around the country.

As Lisa looks back, she seems able to accept what happened, yet she feels enormous sorrow about the energy and anxiety that she, Adam, and their children invested in concealing their secrets. She recalls an evening when she finally told the truth to an old, old friend from the city where she lived with Adam for so many years. "I said, 'That's my story,' and she said, 'You know, Lisa, everyone in our community has known it for years.'

"We tried to disguise ourselves," she concludes, "but everybody knew and I think maybe we wanted them to know. The burden was so heavy."

Mac

Mac Harper is a gay father. He too has known anxiety, depression, and the torn feeling of leading two lives. He knows about the overwhelming tension involved in concealing not just where he was and with whom, but what he feels and who he really is.

Born in 1941, Mac grew up in the Pacific Northwest, where he lived until he left for college eighteen years later. During all that time he was completely unaware that he knew any gay people at all.

Mac's father had led pack trips through the Cascade Mountains as a young man, and helped bring in on horseback some of the first telephone equipment to hit that part of the country. His mother was born in Wyoming, on a ranch about a day's ride from the nearest grocery store. Her family eventually moved into Newcastle, where her father ran an ice company and later a grocery store.

Referring to a Thomas Mann novel about a dynasty of robber barons and powerful merchants that ends up with a frail, pointy-headed intellectual sort of offspring, Mac says, "In many ways I feel like the Hannah Buddenbrook of my family."

Those two very Western and, in a way, very macho traditions converged in Mac, an Eastern intellectual, a top medical school graduate who today is a well-known, well-respected science writer.

The first and only child, Mac was born following a series of miscarriages. His parents divorced when he was four. "Divorce was unusual then," he comments, "and so I grew up in part thinking that I was odd and in part thinking that I had a quasi-secret of my own to keep, although in fact I didn't. But it was a kind of funny mark to have."

Mac remembers at about this same time traveling to Wyoming by train to visit his mother's relatives for Christmas. He recalls the return trip clearly, because there were lots of soldiers on the train and they were kind to him. As they approached his home town, he remembers asking his mother if his father would be there to meet them at the station. She said, "No, he won't. He's not going to live with us anymore." That was the first he heard of his parents' separation and subsequent divorce. He doesn't think he felt particularly unhappy about it at the time, although later it would sadden him as he came to see it as a stigma.

His father, a CPA who did a lot of work for the government during the war, was away from home a lot so Mac was accustomed to his absence. He and his mother moved to a tiny house near the small college where she taught and where she remained until Mac was fifteen. After that she taught in the sprawling high school he attended before he left the West Coast for college.

After the divorce, his mother, who was not a warm person, became very depressed. Mac describes the feeling of "being held at arm's length," and as a result he grew up "with a lot of expectations about being good and self-sufficient," he says. She was, he thinks, very much a woman of her times in that she believed strongly that "she shouldn't raise a momma's boy." His mother also held "outrageously high academic standards" for him, which he almost always met.

"My father was around," Mac adds, "and I saw him, but he was a bit remote to me. He really didn't know how to deal with this kid who wasn't like the son he'd imagined having." His father had left his mother in order to marry another woman. He was an alcoholic as well as something of a workaholic, and very much influenced by Raymond Chandler and Dashiell Hammett.

"I sort of grew up with the image of him as a perfectly awful person," Mac muses, "but I think there were extenuating circumstances. Talk about family secrets. Shortly after my mother died (in the 1980s), a close friend of hers, an elderly maiden lady, told me something I had never known. She said that after I was born my mother refused to have intercourse with my father—forever. Although my mother had told me that they fought only once, she never told me what they fought about. I can imagine now." He thinks that the friend told him the secret because she wanted to "rehabilitate my father, so that he wasn't the bad guy in my eyes."

As Mac mulls over his childhood experiences, he acknowledges that he often felt a pull between what he felt he was supposed to be and what he felt he was. Although it would be many years before he identified himself as gay, he notes that "I certainly had some glimmer of my sexuality from fairly early on, but it was so confused with the generalized unacceptability of sexuality anyway, that I felt in part disbelieving. Partly I didn't have any models, partly I just wanted to keep it at arm's length. But, as many men will say, from the time I was four or five I had some conception of what I was responding to and that it was forbidden."

Shortly after his parents separated an episode occurred that may have contributed to some of his early ideas about secrecy and sexuality. He remembers that a fair amount of sex play went on in the neighborhood and that at some point the adults tuned in to this. He was only four or five and the sex play involved both boys and girls.

"I can remember my mother being furious," he recounts, "and spanking me with a metal spoon—the worst spanking I ever got. And my memory is that it went on and on."

Later in the year, he and his mother moved to the house nearer her job and he was convinced that part of the reason they relocated was because of his being involved in the sex play and the humiliation that caused her. To this day, he cannot say that memory was erroneous.

The incident, he says, "may have played into my idea about what happens when things get out. I suspect that the practical reasons for moving were most important, but my perception was that we moved because we'd lost standing."

Clearly labeled as a smart kid early on, Mac skipped a grade in elementary school. After that, he always felt as though he were struggling to keep up. Making friends was difficult too, but as he got older, he managed to find a group of kids who saw themselves as intellectuals, and finding companions became easier.

When he was barely fifteen, Mac got a job working in the public library, where he also found friends. "At one point," he recalls, "I got involved in kind of a little casual sex play with one of the boy pages who also worked there. It was sort of a momentary thing and it seemed like something he invited. But I remember later on a friend let me know very casually that word had gotten around. I remember being frightened by that. I think it was sort of a veiled warning."

Mac was in high school then, and he would take girls out because it was important to do that. But as he explains, he did it "in a very retarded sort of way."

High school was a huge, rambling place built in the style of a Loire Valley chateau. Mac graduated at the top of a senior class of nearly seven hundred students and was accepted at four prestigious colleges. He chose Harvard, and at seventeen he left the Northwest, alone. All night and much of the next day he flew across the country by propeller plane, to arrive at a school which he had never visited, three thousand miles from his home.

As he looks back on his decision, he says that it was greatly influenced by his relationship with Betty, one of his mother's prize students, and her husband, Jean. It was Betty who said, "Well, if you don't go to Harvard you'll always wonder what it would have been like."

Jean, who was about fifteen years older than Mac, was also a very powerful influence on his life. "He was tough-minded and scary," Mac says. "He knew a lot about opera and music generally, and about literature. He was one of the first people to give me permission to be intellectual, or who even gave me a model I could work towards in that sense. As a sort of nearsighted, academically competent kid in a big public high school, there were times when I really needed that."

At that time Mac had no conception that Jean, who fathered two children before he divorced his wife and who later died of AIDS, was gay.

Mac arrived in Cambridge in the fall of 1958 and settled into school, where he did well. "I went through college unaware that I knew a single gay person," he says, particularly striking in that he was assigned to Adams House, a residence hall known for its large gay population. "I remember saying to someone, probably when I was a freshman, 'Gee, I like this place. It's strange, but it feels like coming home.' Which now seems to me like a loaded thing to say."

Although he was honest enough with himself to know where his sexual interest lay and what he would respond to, he did not accept the identity of being a gay person for many years. "I thought it was something that would pass, that it was a phase," he says. The idea was so unacceptable that he willed himself to ignore his impulses, to reshape himself. "I might have crushes on college friends," he explains, "but they would take the form of sort of intense friendships." He also formed close friendships with women, and although he went through college dating very little, he did have one heterosexual relationship. "It was awkward and I was unhappy and scared about it afterwards, and kind of avoided the girl who was involved," he says. He had no sexual encounters with men.

After he graduated he returned home and passed a dreary summer before returning to Cambridge, deciding that was the place he wanted to stay. He got a job at Harvard's Widener Library. He also started doing some freelance writing and met his future wife in the course of one of his projects. Feeling depressed, he started seeing a psychiatrist who, he says, "avoided dealing with questions of my sexuality—as I did. He colluded with me."

While Mac was in therapy, he made two decisions: to marry Sophie, and to go to medical school.

"From the beginning," he muses, "our marriage was complicated, but in some ways it was a very good one. I actually cared enormously for my wife and still do. She's a comfortable person to be around. She feels real, and I can talk to her. We were scrappers while we were married. We'd get into quarrels, sometimes around other people, but we kept on going and took care of each other. Sex at first was okay, but didn't really work over time. It kind of dwindled off, although Rachel was born in the sixth year of our marriage."

By the time Rachel was born, Mac had struggled through medical school and had taken a position in a research lab. He took it partly because he didn't want to be sent to Vietnam and partly because he had found the practice of medicine generally to be quite frightening. "I think that had I gone on another year, I might have stayed in clinical practice," he says. "I might have gotten more confident. But as it was, I went into a laboratory. It was in that phase that I realized what I really wanted to do was be a writer."

Acknowledging the fact that he wanted to write, not to doctor, was a significant step in honing his professional identity, just as coming to terms with his sexuality would lead eventually to a process of accepting facets of himself that as a child he had been taught were inadmissible.

"It was around the time Rachel was born," Mac explains, continuing his story, "that I had my first sexual encounter with another man. Then the secret life really began." Up to that point, the secrecy had been largely psychological, concealing his feelings rather than his behavior.

By now it was 1969 and sexual mores were starting to loosen up. The gay world was becoming increasingly visible and more accessible. Mac's initial homosexual contacts were made in the "combat zone," a sleazy part of the city known for its pornographic movie theaters and bookstores. "I was browsing in a dirty bookstore," he says, describing his first incident, "and some guy came in and cruised me. We left the store together, went off in a car, did it, and parted."

It wouldn't be until many years later that he had sex with a man he knew. In the beginning, it was always strangers.

During those years Mac felt horrible about what he was doing. He kept telling himself that he had to get this out of his system, that it was just an experience and he had to know what it was like. He also recognized that doing something dangerous was part of the excitement.

"I was absolutely terrified of being discovered," he says. "I was convinced that I would kill myself if I were found out. As a lab worker and a doctor," he continues, "I usually had pills or something that I could have used."

For six years he led a double life. "Essentially," he says, "I had sex with men without talking to them." But everything started to break down for him when he was picked up by someone friendly and vivacious, who was quite a bit younger than he.

"We went back to his place," Mac remembers, "and afterwards he started talking to me and gave me a back rub. And instead of this anonymous kind of utilitarian sex, it turned into something pleasant and friendly and even a little exuberant."

That was the point at which Mac realized he couldn't tolerate the duplicity anymore. He began to see how lonely he had made himself, and realized that he could no longer isolate his sexuality from the rest of his life.

Not long after that, Mac and Sophie, who had been arguing more and more, had a huge fight and decided to separate. Rachel was six.

"Our sexual relationship had continued to deteriorate after Rachel was born," he explains. "We were very affectionate in many ways and we always slept together, but the sex just wasn't working." Because they did things together, shared many values, and had good friends in common, it was, he says, "pretty devastating when we separated. I perceived it, as she did, as a very large loss."

As Mac explains, the fear he had while leading a double life, a fear which was in some ways accurate, was that he would lose a home. He also stresses that for the first few years of his marriage, "The duplicity was completely internal. I felt I'd put my homosexual exploration behind me, which was wrong, but I believed it."

Mac was in a no-win, damned if you do, damned if you don't situation. Unable to combine social and erotic experiences, he felt a complete dichotomy in his emotional life. Even when he started to come out in behavior, the pressure didn't abate because the need for secrecy limited the people with whom he could have sexual encounters. And he felt forced into keeping those encounters from evolving into emotional attachments. The result, he says, was a series of tawdry if exciting experiences.

Mac went into therapy immediately after his separation from Sophie. Within weeks, he mustered the courage to return to Sophie's house to tell her the truth. At the time, they were still talking about reconciliation. Without going into lurid details, he told her much of what had happened over the past six years. She reacted with a mixture of compassion and outrage. She felt terribly hurt and betrayed, but did not show surprise. That was fourteen years ago.

Asked about Sophie now, Mac says, "She always sensed that I was somewhere else, that I wasn't there. And I think that had to do with the sense of duplicity, that there was a secret and she wasn't in on it, perhaps more than the sexuality itself."

After the confrontation, Mac felt awful, but tremendously relieved that the secrecy was over. Yet from another perspective, it wasn't. Sophie was very reluctant for him to come out. At each stage in the process of his becoming more public about his sexual identity, there would be some sort of fight over whether or not people really needed to know. Sophie pressured him to collude with her in maintaining the secret, but Mac never cooperated very much. "I thought the demand she was making was an understandable demand, but not a fair one," he says, "and I didn't comply particularly." For Mac, being forthright was particularly important because for awhile after the separation he was viewed as an eligible bachelor, an awkward situation which he felt compelled to clarify.

Mac and Sophie told Rachel they were getting divorced because they were fighting so much, not getting along. Mac moved into a small apartment nearby and they developed a very regular routine, with Rachel spending several days a week with him, slightly more with Sophie. While Rachel always tried very hard to be fair to both her parents, Mac and Sophie didn't really give her much option for making decisions as to where to be and when, or with whom to spend holidays.

"I had certain views about how these things ought to be done," Mac explains. "That children shouldn't be put in a position of choosing. That the grown-ups were responsible for making the schedule and making it equitable and so forth."

In the year following "the telling and the separating," Mac suffered a fairly severe depression. He continued with a therapist who, he says, supported "the notion that one needed to feel loved and have a sexual outlet," and who was able to help him separate neurotic issues from lifestyle choices. Also during this time, Mac was involved in a chaotic affair with a younger man of whom he was very fond, which lasted about a year.

"He was always trying to go straight," Mac recalls, "and I was less and less concerned about that." Shortly afterward, he met a young lawyer with whom he had what he considers a very constructive relationship.

"Brad helped to solidify my sense of identity," he says. "I remember him saying that if he were asked, 'If you could take a pill and change your sexual identity, would you do it?' he would say, 'No, it would be like killing myself.' He said, 'I have no idea who I would be if I weren't like this.' The sort of strength that I got from him is something that I value to this day."

In the long run, Brad's excessive drinking led to their break up, but it was during the relationship with Brad that Mac came out to Rachel.

Sophie was becoming increasingly aware that knowledge of Mac's being gay was not going to stay confined the way she had hoped it would. She eventually agreed that Rachel needed to hear something, and that it would be best if she heard it first from her father. Mac was working as an editor by that time. He remembers spending a Saturday afternoon discussing what to tell Rachel with Sophie and a couple of friends, including a psychologist who had been through a divorce of his own.

"One of the things he said that was so important," Mac recalls, "is that you always have to leave the door open to talk about it some more. He said, 'She may not take advantage of it, but she needs to know that it's okay to talk about it again later.' "

As he thought about this, Mac began to realize that one of the things he most held against his own parents, particularly his mother, "was this notion that there were things that couldn't be spoken of and were, therefore, unspeakable."

Rachel was about eight when Mac told her they needed to have a talk, that there was something she needed to know. As Mac recalls, he sat down at one end of the couch and she curled up at the other end.

Growing up in Cambridge in the 1970s, Rachel, says Mac, already knew that there were some men who felt closest to other men and related to them best. "I don't know exactly how I told her," he says, "because we didn't talk about sexual mechanics of course, or what people do. But I think I may have said, 'You've heard words like "gay" and "queer" and some of them aren't nice. Well that's what we're talking about.' She put on all the wisdom of an eight year old, nodding 'yes, yes,' and not saying much. She gave very little evidence of being upset. She was wise and absorbent. I told her it would be okay for us to talk about it more if she wanted to, but she rarely did after that."

Rachel, now twenty, describes the scene a little differently. "I don't remember how old I was," she muses, "but I remember not being old enough to know what the word 'gay' meant." She remembers her father telling her that he wanted to have a talk. "I said, 'What about?' And he said, 'Big stuff.' " The two went out onto the screened porch, as she recalls it, and "Daddy said, 'I'm homosexual,' and I said, 'What's that?' I think he must've answered, 'It means you love people of your own sex.' " Then he asked her if she was going to cry.

Rachel remembers wondering why on earth he expected her to weep. "It just wasn't an issue yet," she explains. "It was something I had never heard of. Kids I went to school with didn't say 'faggot' or anything like that. So at that point what he was saying was a completely neutral statement. I don't remember thinking it was any big deal," she continues, "but at the same time, it must've occurred to me that because he was making a big deal, it was a big deal."

The conversation was short and Rachel agrees with her father that she didn't feel upset. The information was delivered as a statement of fact. She knew the door was open, should she have questions, but she doesn't recall having any for a long time after. It did not occur to her until much later to tie the information to her parents' divorce.

Mac found no discernable change in his relationship with his daughter after disclosing his secret. "She wasn't frightened," he says. "She didn't want to talk about it anymore. She just wanted to go back to doing her own thing." On the other hand, he found very little indication that she had dealt with it.

Not long after he told her, however, Mac heard from a neighbor about an incident that happened in an after-school art class her children attended along with Rachel. It seems that a couple of little boys in the class were making up fag jokes and Rachel turned to them and said, "Look, my father is gay and I don't think that's funny." Rachel never mentioned the incident to him. "I guess she did have a fair amount of confidence," Mac observes, adding that for the most part, she has not really wanted anyone but close friends of hers to know.

From Rachel's point of view, "The issues were never so much with my father as with other kids." At the time she learned her father was gay, she attended a protected, "politically correct" private school, where she felt safe from derogatory remarks. From 5th to 8th grade she attended public school, and the situation was quite different. "I was with a very mixed bunch of kids then," she says, "and that was when all the faggot jokes started. This was gay, that was gay. They may have meant 'stupid,' they may have meant 'weird,' they may not have known what they were saying, but the point is the words were there and it made me uncomfortable. I would never use those words."

It was at this time that she began to feel that she was keeping a secret, because she didn't feel able to let kids and teachers know what was bothering her. She did, however, tell some of her closest friends.

"I think I told people when I felt it was necessary," she says. "When they stayed overnight and saw that my father shared a bedroom with another man, for example. Either I told them or they would guess, and I always tried to preempt the guess by telling them because I preferred that to any kind of speculation, to saying anything behind my back."

Rachel met Brad and, as Mac puts it, "although she thought he was distinctly odd, as indeed he was, she liked him." In fact, she still sees him from time to time.

Shortly afterward, Mac met Karl and embarked on a year-long Boston/New York commuting affair which he refers to as "one of the happiest times in my life." Then Karl gave up his job working for an insurance company and moved to Boston, squeezing into Mac's tiny apartment, determined also to make a career as a writer. Rachel was living with him several days a week at the time and he thinks there were instances when she felt envious of his new roommate, although the two got on well.

Rachel agrees that she liked Karl enormously but she also confirms the jealousy her father suspected. She remembers going to New York City with her father to celebrate her ninth birthday and feeling annoyed that Karl was included in the celebration. "I felt it wasn't fair," she says, "and that my birthday belonged to me, but he was making me share it with someone else. And I remember him saying that this was the way things were going to be, that Karl was part of our lives." She is quick to observe that her jealousy had little to do with her father being gay. It was, she says, the kind of jealousy that a child is likely to experience whenever a parent is romantically involved with someone else.

For himself, Mac says, "I would feel torn in that classic kind of way between the partner and the child."

Karl stayed four years. By and large it was a contented, productive time, but he was in many ways a difficult person. And while Mac was devoted to him, Karl was also involved with other men. Finally he got restless and moved to the West Coast. When the relationship ended, Mac remembers this detail: "Rachel said, 'Well it was pretty one-sided wasn't it?' So she was not unaware."

During those four years, Rachel had close friends who would come to the apartment and join in activities with both Mac and Karl. And although Mac hasn't had a long, live-in relationship since, there have been close relationships with other men throughout Rachel's teenage years. "She's known them and dealt with them," he says. "We've all done things together and sometimes they've done things just with her."

Mac came out fairly quickly after separating from Sophie. After years of concealment, it was vital to him that he be up-front about his sexual identity.

As for Rachel, Mac never asked her to conceal his being gay in any way. "I gave her the option of how she would handle it," he says. "Her privacy was her privacy and the strain was really that she, and even more her mother, were concerned that I would do public things, like go on national television or radio." Mac did do a brief stint as a health commentator on a national television show, but that didn't focus on his being gay, which is what they were worried about.

When Rachel was fourteen, however, he was asked to chair a gay and lesbian forum, which was actively lobbying for nondiscrimination policies regarding sexual orientation. He asked Rachel how she felt about it, telling her that he'd been asked to do it and that it seemed very important to him. As he recalls, she said it was fine with her. Sophie, however, objected and got very upset. "She felt that this was going to be too public," Mac explains, noting they still lived within a few blocks of each other. "We had a few fights about it," he remembers, "but I went and did it anyway, arguing that it was a pretty invisible type of position."

According to Mac, "That was one of the times Rachel felt caught between her parents. Her mother didn't want me to do it and I wanted to do it. And it was hard for her. She would have less control over the information than she was used to having. If she had said no, I would not have done it, but essentially, she gave me permission to do it." He adds that if his daughter had objected and if he had then refused the position, he doesn't know that he necessarily would have told her he had forgone it on her account. He would have found another way to explain his choice, so that she would not feel she had prevented him from doing something he wanted to do.

Rachel remembers the incident surrounding her father's decision to lead the forum somewhat differently and with lingering resentment. "He asked my permission," she says, "and I told him no, that I didn't want him to do it. And neither did my mother. We both felt it was too visible and that a lot of people that we hadn't told would suddenly know. I didn't know if it would necessarily be a problem at school, but I didn't want to deal with it. And that was a very, very bad situation. He didn't speak to me for a couple of days. He was very mad at me. Then he gave me a long lecture about how he thought queer-bashing was wrong. I finally said, 'Fine, go ahead and do what you want.' And he did. He got his way. What I was really thinking was, 'Yes, I agree with you, it has to be stopped. But I don't want you to do it, because it affects my life.' I felt like I had been punished for giving him the wrong answer."

At twenty, Rachel sees her father's involvement in gay causes differently. He participates in the Gay Pride march and openly supports gay organizations. "None of that bothers me now," she says, adding, "I'm proud of him for those things, actively proud, but I would never tell him that because I'm not very demonstrative."

As Mac looks back over his experience with his daughter, he seems satisfied with the way he handled it. "I think telling Rachel is one of the few instances where I feel fairly secure about what happened, that it was an appropriate time for her, that it was important to open it up and talk about it, but not to force her to talk about it. My impression is that for her, as for most children of married gay parents, the divorce was a larger and more painful issue than my sexuality, that emotionally she can deal with my sexuality more comfortably than with the pain of losing her family and her sense of home."

Rachel agrees completely with her father that her parents' divorce was a much bigger issue to her than learning that he is gay. Although she commends her parents for never badmouthing each other and for sharing her generously, although she feels they did the best they could to be certain she always had two parents, she cannot dismiss the strain associated with her living arrangements following the divorce.

"For so long, it was such an effort to just sort of keep things together. This business about going back and forth between houses was really damaging because they have very different lifestyles. At my mother's I was a slob. Everybody eats out of the refrigerator. At my dad's house, we'd have breakfast together with silverware. You don't leave a sock or a magazine on the floor or you're an evil person."

As she has grown older and has created some distance between herself and her parents, living away at college for a large part of the year, Rachel has done a lot of thinking about what the divorce meant in her life and how it has affected her ideas about her parents. She and her father, she says, "have never had a discussion about how hard it must've been for him to decide to come out, how sad it must have made him. We haven't discussed how guilty and angry he must've felt towards himself, because I'm sure that even if he knows that he's not responsible and that he's done nothing wrong, you could say in some way that his being gay is what caused their separation or caused the problems that led to their separation."

Looking back to the years before he came out, Mac says, "You know, in order to be good at deception, you have to be good at self-deception, and I was certainly able to do that. I kept believing it wasn't true somehow. I think there's a funny kind of depersonalization that goes on through all that. It's as though you simply don't connect to the world. You're not part of it." For Mac, sharing his secret with his wife and daughter opened the door to the truth. Yes, it led to the end of his marriage, the dissolution of his family and home as he had worked to make them, but without that pain, he would have lost himself. Without that disclosure, his daughter would never have really had the opportunity to know who her father is.

Rachel continues that thought. For her, the fact that her father is gay is, as she explains, "a part of something that shaped me, and eventually anyone who is close to me will end up knowing, just for that reason."

When Rachel was seventeen she went to France for a year to work as an au pair. There she became involved with a Frenchman several years older than she, eventually moving into his apartment. When she came back to the U.S., Felix came to visit. He got along beautifully with her father, despite the fact that their communication was limited, since Felix speaks no English and Mac knows little French.

Rachel had never mentioned to Felix that her father was gay, but during the three-week-long visit she decided she wanted to let him know because "it was a piece of my life that was missing." Knowing that Felix is more conservative than she is, Rachel worried that he would take the revelation poorly. She knew too that she was not willing to make a stand, to say, "Accept this or forget me."

One day they were sitting together in a restaurant and as a waiter walked by, Felix said musingly, "Do you think he's gay or straight?" Rachel felt as though her chair had been pulled out from under her. "It was odd," she says, "because that's a question my father and I will ask each other. We make jokes about it." When Felix posed the question, however, she didn't know if it conveyed a value judgment. "I couldn't tell where he was coming from," she continues, "so I said, 'You know, my father is gay.' He said, 'Really?' He sounded as though he were very surprised and very amazed, but not the least bit critical."

Several minutes later, after reassuring Rachel that he felt no animosity toward gay people, Felix added that if it were his father, he didn't think he could ever accept it. "You would have had to," Rachel responded, "because you have no choice. It's either that or you don't have a father."

"One of the chronic problems for me as well as her at this point," Mac says, "is whether you bother making a production out of telling people. I almost wish it were in my personal style to wear an earring or something like that, just so I wouldn't have to worry." Mac operates under the assumption that people know that he's gay, but from time to time he realizes that's not always true. For the most part it isn't a problem for him because he has created enough publicity that when people introduce him, they just kind of make the information part of their introduction. For Rachel, the situation is trickier. Each time she becomes close to someone new, she has to make a decision whether or not to let people know.

Rachel is convinced that her father told her his secret at the right time, in the best way possible.

"I'm glad that he waited until he understood himself, until he had given a label to what he was, but I'm also glad he didn't wait much longer because then I think I would have felt as if something had been withheld from me. And you don't really know somebody if you don't know a part of them." Having grown up with the information, she is able to integrate it with other events in her life.

One aspect of her parents' divorce and her dual living situation that Rachel thinks has made her life easier is that she has defined her parents as sexual beings from an early age. She can remember going into her mother's room one night and seeing another shadow in her bed. "I knew who he was and I knew what was going on, and I can remember a sort of sick, 'How dare she!' feeling." She also remembers understanding that her father and Karl shared a sexual relationship.

"What all this meant," she observes, "is that from an early age I had their sexuality cleared up and accepted. And I feel like, if I'm going to accept theirs, they're going to accept mine. That's all there is to it."

When Rachel is involved with a man sexually, she talks about it and feels no compulsion to hide their relationship. When she brought Felix home, she says her parents were upset and surprised. "I sort of hit them over the head with it," she says, "but there was no way I was going to pretend to be something I wasn't, when they weren't doing any pretending. So that's a good side of it: nobody's fooling anybody."

If Rachel has children of her own and her father is involved in an intimate relationship with another man, she thinks that she would be clear with her child right from the start "that this is the person granddad loves, the person he shares his life with."

Leanne

Leanne Franklin is a gay mother with a seven-year-old son, Keith. Keith has another mother too, Barbara Sammis. Leanne, who teaches psychology at a community college, and Barbara, a therapist, live together with Keith in a working-class neighborhood in a suburb of Washington, D.C. In their mid-forties, both have been married and divorced.

Leanne and Barbara have lived together as a gay couple for the past eighteen years. They adopted Keith when he was eight months old. Their story is different from the two we have just heard because from the start they have been clear with Keith, not only that he is adopted, but that he has two mommies and that they are gay.

"About ten years ago," Leanne begins, "Barbara and I started talking about adding a child to our family. We made several attempts at alternative insemination—some people call it artificial insemination, but really, there's nothing artificial about it. We used different donors, some we knew and some through a sperm bank, but none of that took so we decided to go the adoption route."

Legally, she explains, two women can't adopt a child but a single woman can. That meant that either she or Barbara had to be the legal adoptive parent. When asked which one assumed that role, Leanne replies, "It's kind of irrelevant, isn't it?" It is the same answer she gave when asked which partner received the inseminations. She adds that Keith doesn't know either, because it's not meaningful to his experience right now. What is important to him is that he has two mothers.

Leanne and Barbara arranged the adoption through a woman named Diane who was involved in finding homes for Peruvian babies. When the two went through the adoption process, they did not tell Diane or their lawyer that they are a gay couple. They figured the less information they offered, the less they would have to lie.

Part of the process involved having a social worker visit them at their home. "We used a social worker who was a friend of ours." Leanne explains. "I don't think she had to say anything dishonest in her report, but she didn't say everything. Going through a social worker we didn't know, we would have had to make up a phony separate bedroom and we just couldn't see ourselves doing that. We just couldn't see ourselves lying that way."

Once the preliminary arrangements were made, Leanne and Barbara traveled to Peru together, where they met Diane, who acted as their interpreter, and the lawyer who managed the legal work. One of them presented herself as the adoptive mother and the other as her friend, there to offer support.

If Keith had been conceived through artificial insemination, however, Leanne says it would have been important to him to know who his biological mother was. "It becomes part of his story," she says, "the story about his birth. In the adoption story, it seems kind of irrelevant which one of us signed the papers. What's important was that we both went to the foster home where Keith was."

The person who is not the legal parent, Leanne explains, carries a power of attorney written by the legal parent, giving her full authority to make decisions regarding Keith's health care in the event the legal parent is unavailable. Leanne and Barbara also wrote a contract that states their firm understanding that they are both Keith's parents.

"I don't think the contract actually has any legal weight," Leanne comments. "It's just designed to illustrate to a judge, if we were to separate, that our intention was that we are both parents. We're a family, with two parents."

Leanne and Barbara began telling Keith the story of his adoption even before he had any real understanding of language. "We tell him," Leanne says, "how we were a couple and we wanted to have a baby and we couldn't have a baby ourselves. We contacted a woman named Diane who lived in Peru and knew that there were some babies there that needed families. We wrote to her and said we wanted a baby and asked if she knew of any babies that needed families. And she wrote back that yes, there was a little baby there, a little boy, who needed a family."

She continues the story, telling it as she tells it to Keith. "We got on a plane and went there. We got off the plane in Peru and Diane picked us up and we went to the home where the little boy was living with some very nice people, the Castenadas. Their job was to take care of kids who were waiting for families and they had had this baby for four months."

Of course, the little boy was Keith. She continues, explaining that they tell Keith how cute he was and how there were lots of cats running around. "We tell him," Leanne says, "how we knew immediately when we saw him that he was the perfect baby for us. And we talk about how the first day or so he was a little sad because he was separated from these very nice people whom he obviously loved."

Leanne and Barbara have kept a family photo album right from day one. Their album begins with pictures of Keith with his foster family in their home. Then there are pictures of the hotel where Leanne, Barbara, and Keith stayed before leaving Peru.

When they arrived back in the United States three weeks later, Barbara's parents met them at the airport for a warm reception. When they got home, the neighbors came over to see the new baby. Some of them praised Leanne and Barbara for taking in a poor third world baby who would otherwise be out on the street. Others were just happy to have another kid on the block.

Several weeks after they brought Keith home, they had a big party, inviting about a hundred people, including many neighbors. Yet Leanne is quick to say that while people in the neighborhood are friendly with each other, they tend to be acquaintances, not friends.

"It's unclear to me what the neighbors make of us," she observes. "I can't say that we've ever sat down with anyone on the street and said, 'As gay parents, we . . .' or, 'As a gay couple, we . . .' But it's very clear to them that Keith is being raised by two women, both of whom he thinks of as his mother."

As a gay couple, Leanne says, she and Barbara are not interested in making a statement about their personal lives by wearing t-shirts that say "I'm a dyke and proud of it" or inserting gay rights issues into every possible conversation. On the other hand, they don't keep up a front by having separate bedrooms and only allowing their very closest friends to know that they are gay. "We're in the middle," she says, "where basically everyone we're friendly with and probably everyone we work with knows we're gay."

They do, however, participate in Gay Pride marches and they take Keith along. "It's important for him to know about the politics of being gay," Leanne says. "He needs to know about human rights and the gay rights that have been won and that some people don't like gay people. It's part of his political education. It's also part of developing a group identity. I think at some point he has to know that we have a connection to other gay people in a way that we don't have to straight people. And that this is a part of who we are, even though it's not a big public part."

When Leanne and Barbara embarked on their shared motherhood, they were entering relatively uncharted territory. They knew lesbian couples where one of the partners came to the relationship with a biological child. But they didn't know any couples who had gone about it their way, jointly taking on responsibility for a child in a sort of dual motherhood.

"At the time," Leanne says, "we thought, well a kid can't have two mothers. No one had a mommy 1 and a mommy 2. So the only thing we were clear about, and in retrospect I think we were wrong, was that he shouldn't call us both 'Mom.'"

As it happened, Keith took care of that dilemma on his own. He started calling Leanne "Lea," his way of trying to say Leanne, and he called Barbara "Mom." "Although," Leanne observes, "when he's alone with me, he tends to call me 'Mom.' He's kind of flexible about it. He differentiates when he's with both of us, but he goes back and forth."

In the years that have passed since they adopted Keith they've met other lesbian couples with children who call both their parents "Mom," or in one instance, "Mommy" and "Mama."

"I guess we were wrong thinking it was impossible for a kid to have two moms," Leanne laughs. "I mean, we knew that we could both mother him, but we didn't know if he could conceptually call us both moms, but it seems like he can, and other kids have done the same."

When Keith began attending preschool at the college where Leanne works, the staff knew her and knew that she was gay. "We were very open there," she says. "We said 'We're a family and Keith has two mothers.' We never said 'We're a lesbian couple and our child is enrolled in your center so now you have a lesbian couple,' but it was obvious that's the way it was."

When Keith entered the local public school for kindergarten, Leanne and Barbara found themselves confronting a very different situation. Keith's legal mother took him to registration, and his other mother's name went on the form as his guardian.

"We told his teacher," Leanne says, "that Keith has two mothers. Because what we didn't want was to have the teacher say anything to make him doubt the validity of his own experience. We didn't want the teacher to say, 'Don't be ridiculous; you can't have two mothers.' His version of the world needed to be preserved."

Despite their conversation with Keith's teacher, Leanne and Barbara felt that they needed to be very low key about being gay. Not only was Keith different because he had two mommys, but every other child in his class came from an intact, white family. Perhaps it was because his family structure differed from the norm, perhaps it was because he was a Latino kid—Leanne isn't sure—but halfway through the school year, she and Barbara began to realize that the teachers held only minimal expectations for Keith.

They decided to apply to a private school. Keith was admitted and given a generous scholarship, but even so, Leanne and Barbara were really going to have to stretch to come up with tuition. "We knew," Leanne says, "that if we were going to be paying a lot of money for an alternative school, we were going to be up-front and honest. We said, 'Keith is different in a number of ways. He's Peruvian, he's adopted, he's Jewish, and he's got two mothers and this is who we are.'

"The admissions director said, 'Fine. We really want Keith,' " Leanne continues. "She also said, 'We've never encountered this situation before exactly. If anybody at the school is the least bit insensitive to your family situation, I hope you'll tell us.' So that was pretty fantastic." Keith has been at the school two years now and he is flourishing.

When it comes to deciding whether or not to tell people that they are gay, Leanne and Barbara make their decision based on the particular situation. Yet they have never suggested to Keith that he should conceal his two mommies' relationship in any way.

"I know gay women who tell their children not to tell people outside the home that they're lesbians," Leanne says, "and that just violates every assumption I would make about the best way to bring up a kid. You want them not to be ashamed. Telling them not to tell makes them wonder, 'Why can't I tell? Does that mean we're bad?'

"At this point," she continues, "I could say to Keith, 'You know, there are a lot of crazy people out there who don't like gay people.' I would rather say that to him and let him worry a little about that and then make his own decisions about what to say or not say. I know kids who are teenagers now and have gay parents: typically, they tell some people and not others. They're very careful and thoughtful about who they let in on it—who they think can handle it, who they think can't."

Although it has yet to happen, Leanne knows that some day another child may strike out at Keith and say pejoratively, "Hey, your mother's gay!" The possibility doesn't particularly frighten her because she thinks Keith will have the confidence to deflect it.

"Our theory," she explains, "is that he sees our being gay as natural and he sees it as good. If someone makes a nasty remark about it, he'll be mystified by that comment and he'll correct the child by saying something like, 'Well of course my mother's gay. What about it?' He'll have enough confidence in his own experience not to have to be an idealogue about it but it'll be more like, 'Well sure she's gay. That's not bad.' "

6

White Lies and Broken Laws

PARENTS frequently break rules and tell lies. Sometimes we violate formal laws, and sometimes we court dishonesty by ignoring policies in our workplace or by simply not telling the truth. How many of us have hedged on our income taxes, misused a sick day at work, or lied to our children about family finances? When parents break the rules, whether or not they get caught, they risk being sucked up in a whirlwind of lies and cover-ups.

Sometimes we accept the risk deliberately. Weighing our options, we choose the illegal route with full knowledge of the potential consequences should we be discovered. We do it with our eyes open, perhaps because the rule or law seems unjust, perhaps because we feel cornered. At other times, we cross to the dark side of the street by accident, misunderstanding, or poor judgment. However our tap-dance with the line between right and wrong begins, it is likely to launch us on a pattern of deception that seeps over into other parts of our lives and eventually makes its mark on others in the family.

When parents make illegal or unethical choices, they risk losing credibility in the eyes of their children. When parents break rules and conceal behavior, they can alienate, amuse, confuse, humiliate, and sometimes frighten their kids. The extent to which the deceit affects their children depends partly upon the motivation in creating the secret, the persistence in continuing it, and on how directly the information withheld or distorted touches upon the kids themselves.

Children seem to have a much greater capacity to forgive or at least accept their parents' errors when they see them as isolated from the mainstream of family life, as quirks that stand outside a home atmosphere laced with love and a sense of solidarity. When kids incorporate their parents' infractions as another aspect of a household that hangs heavy with half truths and unknowns, they are more likely to react with bitterness or confusion. The less directly the deception affects them as individuals, the less likely they are to feel wronged and resentful.

As with many other types of concealments, the formation of secrets around money, employment, and legal entanglements is often motivated by a desire to protect oneself or one's children—from the shame that accompanies being found out, from the flood of difficult feelings that may well be unleashed when the truth is revealed and, along with it, the fact that there has been concerted deception. When such rationales are given, it is often illuminating to look closer.

Carol

Carol Redmond was brought up in the 1950s in the Chicago area. "My parents were both Jewish," she says. "My mother was nineteen when they got married and my father was twenty-two. He was a Stalinist. He wanted to make it financially but he also wanted it to be a better world. He was really confused." Her mother was a model and she made much more money than her fiancé, which totally threatened him. He wouldn't let her work, which was okay with her. "White picket fence security, that was what my mother hoped for," says Carol, "and boy did she not get it. I mean, what she thought she was getting and what she got were complete opposites."

Carol's father died in 1968, when she was nineteen. For all her criticisms of him and the way he lived his life, it is clear that she remembers him with tremendous affection. "I don't think my father would mind my telling our story," she says. "I think he would just like me to tell it kindly."

She begins by saying that her father had two names, Martin, which he was born with, and Scratch, his nickname. His parents were Orthodox Jews and his mother died when he was two. He was brought up on the West Side of Chicago by his grandparents, very religious Jews, and, explains Carol, "He hated it so much. He reasoned, 'If there is a God, how could he kill my mother when I was a baby?' " When he was about sixteen, Martin's anger exploded and he rejected Judaism in favor of politics.

Carol's mother, Katherine, was born in Poland and came to the U.S. with her Russian parents when she was three. "She always felt like she was an immigrant," Carol explains. "She never got over that—coming to this country and being put in the dumb class in school because she couldn't speak English. She spoke Russian and Yiddish at home." Katherine's family settled on the West Side. Later she met Martin, they fell in love, and they got married.

"We were a wonderful family," Carol reports. "We were 'Father Knows Best.' " George was born first, followed a year later by Carol. After several moves within the city, the family relocated in Skokie, an affluent, mostly Jewish suburb, well launched on an upwardly mobile trajectory. Over the years, three more sons followed.

When Carol was ten, however, her predictable, pretty, privileged world cracked wide open. She was about to have her first big party when her parents told her she couldn't have it because her father had embezzled a great deal of money.

"The problem with the way we lived was that everything about it was a total contradiction," Carol comments. "My father, who was living in the fast lane and trying to make it all happen, was a CPA who was really a songwriter in his heart of hearts. He got in debt over his head and stole $30,000 from some wonderful people who were his clients. That was the beginning of the end for my father and for all of us."

She remembers that her parents sat down together with her and George and explained what had happened. Carol canceled her party. She told her friends she couldn't have it, and she told some of her closest friends why. "I knew what he had done was bad," she says, "but it wasn't bad to me anymore. My whole sense of justice changed. It was like, if my father steals money, then it's okay to steal money. That was the only way I could deal with the fact that he had done something wrong. It all of a sudden became not wrong to do that."

What Carol's parents didn't tell her until many years later was that on the eve of her much-anticipated party her father almost went to jail. "From that point on," she says, "my father's whole life, everything he did, was underground. We never knew what he was up to."

Martin sold the house in Skokie very quickly, way below market value. "That was to pay off the $30,000," Carol explains, "but because he had to do it so fast, he actually lost money. The people he embezzled from had said they would drop the charges if he paid them back."

After frantically unloading the house in Skokie, the family relocated to a bigger, fancier house in Winnetka. "The moment we moved to Winnetka, it was like a new life," Carol says. "We moved up. We rented these fabulous houses and every two years we'd move to more palatial quarters and another child would be born."

From the time they left Skokie until Martin died nine years later, Carol never really knew what her father did for a living. "He would come home at odd hours. He'd do crazy things, like once he brought home a hundred pairs of sneakers. Or he'd come home with a new car three nights in a row. Bizarre things. Fun things. He was a fun guy." Much later she learned that the sneakers came from a factory that had burned to the ground in a suspicious fire that same night.

As Carol looks back on her childhood, she recalls that even when she was very little, "There was always clandestine stuff going on in our house." Martin and Katherine had both joined the Communist party during the early years of their marriage. During the McCarthy era, "People hid out with us," Carol says, "but we were never told much about them." What affected her more directly was that her mother would frequently send George and her off to peace marches and civil rights demonstrations while she stayed home to tend the younger children. "We'd say, 'What are we doing? Where are we going? Why?' But we got very little explanation. We'd be sent on these long bus rides by ourselves, when I was eleven, twelve, and I just remember hating it. It didn't come from my gut. I didn't understand what was going on."

Carol's life had two distinct parts. On the one hand, she was exposed to a bevy of political, social, and artistic experiences. There was always music in the house and her father shared his passion for the theater with his kids, taking them to play after play. On the other hand, she was, by her own admission, a spoiled brat who expected to get whatever she wanted.

"Everything was a fairy tale," she says. "You did something wrong but then it got fixed. So somehow the message to us was, 'Don't worry. Daddy can always make everything alright.' He was everybody's savior, the good guy. But then there was another side to him, the Martin who went off to work and sometimes would get home at three, four in the morning. Some days he would be coming in the door as I was leaving to go to school. 'Working hard . . . tax season. . . .' We never questioned it."

In retrospect, Carol's mother Katherine used her oldest daughter to act out parts of her own life. "My mother was a totally selfish human being," Carol says. "She was sarcastic. She was mean. She used humor to destroy you but I'm not sure she knew she was doing it, and when I was a child growing up in Winnetka, I didn't understand about sarcasm. I thought it was funny."

When Carol was in the ninth grade her mother decided to get an undergraduate degree. Katherine would lock herself up in her room to read Shakespeare and Carol would be responsible for the three younger children. "Whenever I would say, 'I'm not doing this anymore,' she would say, 'Now, now Cinderella.' That was really cruel. Looking at it from a feminist perspective, she was trying to save herself, to get a degree and become a person in the world. But if you look at it from my perspective, she wasn't there for me. *My* schooling went out the window. Sort of like, 'She's the daughter: it doesn't matter.' So to make up for it, I decided to be the most popular kid in the ninth grade, which doesn't happen unless you absolutely *have* to be that."

As Carol tries to reconstruct exactly what her father was doing during those years, she says that it is like putting together the pieces of a puzzle. He went to work for a company called RBT Development Facilities. There was a proper office to go to and indeed, one summer Carol worked as a receptionist there. "My father hired me and fired me," she says. "I didn't know anything about work-ing and I didn't take it seriously. I'd answer the phone with a British accent and then I'd switch it to a French accent. I was obnoxious. I was a spoiled brat. He said, 'Get out of here.' I said, 'But I'm your daughter.' I got out."

The incident symbolizes the dichotomy in Martin's life. Carol talks about what a wonderful father he was, how much time he devoted to his kids, and how he made a point of doing things with each of them separately. Martin wasn't going to let his daughter get away with lousy work habits. On the other hand, when it came to his own ethics and capabilities. . . .

At one point, he was trying to put George, Carol, and Katherine through college all at the same time. "He couldn't do it," Carol says, "he couldn't make it happen. He wouldn't let us know though. He wouldn't share it with us. His manhood was all tied up with being the big provider, and he totally screwed it up. He was doing it for us, but he ruined his life and, consequently, he ruined ours."

What Martin Redmond really cared about was music and the theater. Before he married he dreamed of making a living as a lyricist. He wrote songs and sold some of them, but he didn't earn very much and, saddled with family responsibilities, he soon turned to more conventional work. Carol says, "I think none of my father's life would have been this way if he had done what he actually should have done, which was to be a songwriter. I always think my mother didn't really care about him enough to let him do that. She wanted her security.

"I think my father was the extreme of his generation," she continues. "The saddest part of that generation is that they were so into making it financially that they sold their souls. They became doctors, lawyers, and accountants. But in fact, my father was something completely different. He was a musician, a writer. That was what he was good at and what he loved. He knew that's what he was, but he never let himself be that. Instead, he lived out somebody else's fantasy of security."

After Carol graduated from high school and went off to college in Wisconsin, Martin became ill and moved the whole family into Chicago so that he could eliminate the commute to work. Carol's three younger brothers, who were eleven, ten, and seven years old at the time, became city kids, settling into a comfortable apartment in a good neighborhood. Yet the privileged surroundings did not prevent two of the boys, Jamie and Brett, from dabbling with drugs. Martin used to tell them he'd give up drinking if they gave up dope, but it was always "No deal, Dad," and he and Katherine seemed to have little control of them even though they were just entering their teens.

Two and a half years after the move, Martin died suddenly at forty-nine. He left a life insurance policy for

$17,000, and nothing else. Carol spent the summer pounding the pavement, trying to help her mother find a cheaper apartment for the family. "My mother was a total basket case, only she didn't know it," Carol says. "She was walking down the street one day and she heard a cry and she wondered what it was, and then she realized it was coming out of her own throat."

Jamie and Brett, aspiring teenage musicians, got jobs in clubs, stayed out late, dropped out of school. "They were dealing drugs by then," Carol remembers. "There would be dealers coming to the house at all hours of the night and my mother was like, 'I'm not seeing this. I don't want to know this.'" Desperate for money, Katherine got a job as a teacher in a boys school in the ghetto that was housed in a building without windows and permeated with asbestos. Katherine got breast cancer and lung cancer, and died when she was fifty-nine.

Several years before her death, when Jamie was in his twenties, he read an article in the *Chicago Sun* about organized crime. He recognized one of the men in the story as one of his father's business partners. This happened a couple of times. Soon he began to realize it was more than coincidence.

Jamie mentioned his discoveries to Carol. She too found the names and faces familiar from the past. She began to connect the shadowy figures together with incidents in her childhood that had never made much sense—like the night her father brought home all those sneakers. Jamie and Carol were living over two thousand miles apart by this time, but they had long phone conversations about their family. "We had the same conversation for fifteen years," Carol says. "Who were we? Who was our father? What did he do?" George had married shortly before Martin's death and, Carol says, "We have wedding pictures with all these Mafia people. My brother's wife with her proper Jewish family and then there were these thugs. Ricky the Bull, Mac the Monk: these were the names we grew up with."

With the picture coming into focus, they confronted their mother. "She said," Carol remembers, " 'I can't deny it, but I don't know. I can't say it's the truth.' I don't remember if she ever said, 'You're right. You've got it.' But Jamie knew it was right. We knew that we'd hit it."

The way Carol explains it, before the Mafia makes loans to a family business, they make a careful check of the company's books. As an accountant, Martin would be sent in to scrutinize the records. And when the loan was made and the company was unable to repay it, Martin would be involved in the takeover.

When Carol thinks about how her father's deception affected her family, she focuses first on Martin. "I think my father was a psychopath," she says quietly. "It was really sad. He had two lives, this happy home life in Winnetka and this Chicago fast-track life. He was a great father and he was charming beyond belief but I think his life was cut short because he couldn't continue it."

"What was really going on was that we weren't making it. There was incredible stress. We just didn't have the kind of money you needed for that lifestyle. It's like my father wanted us to have it better than we did, and to believe it. In order to do that, he created a fantasy world. But we were living a lie in Winnetka. I would have preferred to have grown up on the West Side and had it all be real, had him be a struggling songwriter. I would have much preferred that to struggling in Winnetka to be something we weren't.

I would have had a great time in the West End. I didn't need the other kind of experience to make my life better, but he thought we did."

As a reaction to the way her father lived his life, Carol has developed a firm conviction in the rightness of following one's own heart. For her, that means making career and family choices that feel right, with little regard to how they will be perceived by others.

Another part of her father's legacy is her attitude toward money. "My brothers and I are all totally screwed up about money. None of us really have any idea what it is and what you should and shouldn't do with it because it's all a fairy tale. If you make a mistake, you get bailed out."

She recalls a conversation she had once with her future husband, when they were talking about where they would live. Carol said, "Well of course, it's always better to rent than to buy." She remembers her husband looking perplexed. She realizes now that she was parroting a line she heard her father deliver frequently while she was growing up. Now that she knows more about him, she understands that the reason they always rented was tied up with his Mafia dealings. Houses came and went mysteriously, but the next one always seemed grander than the last.

While Carol is adamant that she and her brothers should not and could not have been told the truth about their father's business dealings, she weakens when she focuses on specific instances. Regarding the embezzlement, she says, "It would have been good to know how he solved that problem . . . even if he told us a lie. The way it was, everything just happened by magic."

Andrea

Now twenty-four, Andrea Parrish was only five years old when her father died. She grew up in Michigan with her mother, Stella, and her brother, Warren, ten years her senior.

Social standing was important to Stella, who choreographed a black tie party for her daughter on the occasion of twelve-year-old Andrea's bath mitzvah. At sixteen, Andrea made a striking debutante. When she married in her early twenties, she was poised enough to entertain three hundred guests at an elegant hotel reception.

"But I always suspected something was fishy," she says, looking back on her history. "Whenever I had a chance, I would go through my mother's closets and drawers and try to figure out what the deal was."

Soon after she learned to read, Andrea found a piece of mail addressed to Mrs. Stella Edwards. Her mother's maiden name was Adams and her married name was Parrish. Andrea confronted her mother and grandmother with the letter and they told her it was written to a friend of her grandmother's. A year or so later, she came across a photograph of her mother dressed up in a fancy wedding dress. Stella was alone in the picture, which confused Andrea since she had been told that her parents had a modest wedding and that Stella wore a street dress. Curious, she approached her grandmother who told her that Stella had just dressed up for fun for the portrait. Again, something just didn't ring true. In not telling her the truth, Andrea's mother and grandmother did not realize how richly they had fertilized the young girl's suspicions and undermined her sense of trust in them.

A couple of years later, when she was about nine, Andrea came across a box containing condolence cards and letters and her father's obituary. "That was when I found out that everyone had been married before," she says. "Both my mother and my father."

Later that night, she went off in the car with her brother to pick up pizza. She recalls saying, " 'Warren, what's the deal? I've suspected something for a long time and now I find out this.' " Not only did her brother confirm her discoveries, he went on to tell her that her father, Frank, had been married, not once, but twice before marrying Stella. He explained too that he was from her mother's first marriage, that he was her half, not full brother.

"I think it was very hard for him to tell me," she says, "not because he felt he was betraying our mother but because he was afraid of how I might react, but we had too much behind us for it to matter."

Andrea did not confront her mother with her discoveries at that time. She felt that her mother had lied to her before and that she would probably lie to her again. "I've never really gotten over being pissed off at my mother for not telling me all this before I was old enough to figure it out for myself," she says.

Warren and his natural father had not been in regular contact since well before Andrea's birth. Since he never appeared, there was never any reason for Stella to explain him. Years later, when Andrea was a teenager, the telephone rang and she answered it. The caller asked her to give her mother a message, that Warren's natural father had died. Passing on that information was the first time that Andrea acknowledged to her mother that she knew that she and Warren had different fathers. Stella didn't seem surprised and although she has never discussed it with her brother, Andrea is fairly certain that he had long since told her mother about all her discoveries.

Plagued by a need for more information, Andrea continued to try to ferret out more details about her parents' lives. She learned that her father's first wife was an opera singer. Frank had been passionate about music and had felt he could make a star out of her. When his effort failed, so too did the marriage.

As for Frank's second wife, her mother and grandparents would only say that she was a "floozy."

Andrea also hit a brick wall when it came to getting information about her mother's first marriage. "She definitely acknowledged that she had gotten married before but I'll never get the real story about why they got divorced."

Once when she got mad and yelled at her mother for not telling her that Warren was her half brother, Stella answered tartly that she wasn't old enough to know. Then she switched gears and said that Warren had asked her not to tell. That didn't ring true with Andrea. She says it merely added to the sense of skepticism and disbelief that had been building since she found the box of condolence letters.

"I can't see my mother looking to my brother to make a decision about how to deal with a nine year old," she says. To this day, Andrea remains reluctant to believe anything Stella tells her.

While her parents' previous marriages were probably more important to her than they might have been to other children, in that she had never really known her own father and felt a void in terms of her origins, the secrets Andrea discovered about her parents' marriages and her brother's paternity did not directly affect her life. What they did, she says, was to create an atmosphere of distrust between her and her mother.

Now a young adult, Andrea is on a crusade to find out all she can about her father. In the past few years, she has put tremendous energy into establishing relationships with distant relatives, intent on learning all she can about their recollections of Frank. What she has found so far upsets her, because it contradicts what she was told as a child. "My mother told me that he graduated from Stanford, but one of my older cousins told me that he left school after a few years and never got his degree. So I don't know who's right on that one," she says, citing one example of the sort of discrepancy she has unearthed.

Several years ago, as part of her quest for information, Andrea delved into her mother's papers and came up with her father's will, the contents of which surprised her. When her father died, his will stipulated that his liquid assets be divided between her mother and Warren. What was left to Andrea was his seat on the New York Stock Exchange, which was to be sold, the money liquidated to be placed in a trust fund, which would come to her when she reached twenty-five.

"Well, he didn't have any money when he died, so the seat was his only asset," Andrea explains. The seat was sold and the trust fund was established.

Throughout the years, Stella told Andrea and Warren that the trust fund was left to the two of them, with the principle to be divided evenly when Andrea reached twenty-five. After she read the will, Andrea knew differently. She confronted Stella, who pressured her into complicity, calling upon her compassion for her brother. Andrea was left feeling convinced that Warren would suffer tremendous rejection and hurt if he knew that he was not included.

To this day, Warren believes that half of the trust fund will go to him. Andrea, now on the eve of her twenty-fifth birthday, finds herself in a painful quandary spawned by her mother's deception. When the fund comes due, Stella wants her to go to the bank, remove the money, and have two cashier's checks issued in equal amounts, one for her and one for Warren.

Andrea says that she is not concerned about the money. What tears her up is deciding whether to risk hurting her brother in order to reveal the truth. Her brother, she says, has always felt second class.

"I'm in a really bad position," she explains, "because my mother's told us this lie for years and I don't know if I should be the one to change it. There's enormous pressure on me to continue it. Warren might get suicidal. I don't know if he'd really do it but he's threatened to kill himself before when things got really bad for him. I think he might do it if he found he wasn't left anything, especially since my mother's built it up by lying to him all this time. So it's like a double whammy, being lied to and not inheriting anything. I haven't decided what I'm going to do."

As Andrea discusses her father's will, she points out that Stella has kept other financial secrets from her as well. "My mother always told me that my father didn't believe in life insurance," she says, "but come to find out, he did have a policy. But he had borrowed money from my uncle and it had gotten to the point where the only way he could pay him back was to liquidate the life insurance. So it's not that he didn't have life insurance, but that he spent it while he was still alive."

She continues to explain that she is also the beneficiary of another trust, this one established for her by her paternal grandmother who lived in New York. A couple of years ago Andrea was displeased with the way the trustees were handling the money, and tried to make some changes in its management. Stella told her that she would take care of it by having the trust fund moved to Detroit intact. The money would remain in trust, but she would serve as the trustee.

"The truth was, and she knew this," Andrea explains, "that you can't move a trust fund from one state to another." Eventually, she coerced Stella into admitting that she had planned to liquidate the fund in New York and then move the capital to Michigan, where she would manage it until Andrea reached twenty-five. "That was how she planned it and the only way I figured it out," Andrea says, "was that I called the lawyer in New York who administered it and he said, 'Well, you can't move a trust fund. I told your mother that.' Then I called her and as much as I wanted to scream at her, I said, 'Mother I understand what you did and that you tried to do it to protect me. I just want you to admit it.'" Stella basically confirmed Andrea's statements, but Andrea notes, "She didn't cry or anything. She didn't feel remorseful."

When asked why Stella would try to manipulate the funds behind her back, Andrea says, "She doesn't need the money. What she needs is control over me. She sees me as a rebellious child."

When her great-aunt Agnes, an elderly widow with no children, became seriously ill, Stella befriended her although they had had little contact for many years. Agnes's will called for her estate to be given to charity, but at Stella's urging the terms of the will were changed and Stella was left the lion's share. As Stella explained it, she also begged Agnes to leave a generous chunk of money to Andrea and Warren individually, with herself as the trustee. Stella successfully urged Agnes to structure the trust so that Warren and Andrea wouldn't receive the money until they reached the age of fifty-five. And Stella never even told Andrea that the money existed. She did, however, tell Warren, who decided to tell his sister.

"Warren knew because she tells him everything," Andrea says. "He told me about it, as usual. I think he thought I knew but when he realized I didn't, he told me. I never told my mother I knew. He was mad about the provision that said we had to be fifty-five but he's passive. He doesn't have any fight in him. It was like, 'Maybe I'll be alive and maybe I won't.' "Again, Andrea is convinced her mother withheld the information from her in order to exert a measure of control. She is quick to acknowledge that this is a familiar pattern, that things are told to her brother, but not to her.

"I think my mother favors Warren," she says, "that it's much easier for her to get along with him than with me." By sharing confidences with him, Andrea explains, her mother reinforces that he is the favorite child. "I don't resent him," she says. "I resent her."

Recently married, Andrea now refuses to talk with Stella about money. "She's always asking me what we have in our bank account, what our house cost," she says, "and I won't tell her."

"My mom takes after my grandfather," she observes, "and her love is very conditional. If you don't do things or see things the way she wants you to, then you don't love her."

Andrea says that her mother's many secrets are another form of manipulation and control, reflecting lack of confidence in Andrea's ability to make wise choices. Now, Andrea says she is left seriously doubting her own ability to be a good mother.

"I don't feel like I want to be a mother at all," she says. "I'd like to be able to want children, but it scares me. I hope that changes one day."

7

It Never Happened

KIDS have sensitive antennae. Just as they often intuit when their parents are worried about money or when they are not getting along, they also internalize many other messages. Chief among these is, "That's not something we talk about." Sometimes "that" refers to an unfortunate or embarrassing incident that occurred in the past, such as a business failure or a legal entanglement. Either directly or indirectly, we let our children know that it is not permissible to bring up the time Mommy got arrested for drunk driving and had to go to jail overnight. We do it through direct prohibitions or through menacing glances. We do it by voicing our disapproval or by abruptly shifting the conversation.

Whether we convey our message head on or whether we resort to insinuation, we let our children know that by raising the forbidden issue they are being disloyal. They come to understand that if they break the silence, they betray us. How terribly strong a child must be to risk betrayal of those whom he depends upon for the love, approval, and acceptance that make him feel that he has a safe place in the world.

We parents are powerful figures in our children's lives, and we ought never underestimate the authority they attribute to the messages we send, whether delivered directly or subtly intimated.

The child who is pressed into conspiracy by his parents in order to protect their reputation or the reputation of the extended family is put in an untenable situation. He recognizes the contradiction, he sees that his parents have committed a wrong, but he grows confused as to what really matters. He begins to wonder if appearances are more important than reality. He begins to doubt his own sanity too. Are reputation and image so sacred that they must be preserved at any cost? Is illusion more important than truth?

What are the consequences, then, when a child is the victim of the negative behavior, when the child is himself or herself the substance of the secret that threatens to damage the image of the family?

If my parents choose to protect the image of the family and if I am a sacrifice that has to be made in the process, the child wonders, how can I be worth anything? If they will not listen to me, if they do not hear my cries or if they choose to ignore what they see, who will protect me?

Incest is one of the most horrible family secrets. It renders a child powerless and erodes his or her ability to trust. Yet while it may be more horrifying than most secrets, it has in common with others the fact that it is not the initial molestation in itself that appears to cause the overwhelming distress and desperation. It is the process of pretending it didn't happen, of allowing it to continue, of denying its import and enormity, that is largely responsible for the damage that ensues.

Kevin

When Kevin Rath tries to describe the secrets in his family, he runs into difficulty because there are so many to choose from. In trying to put them under one blanket, he points to a pattern of alcohol abuse and sexual abuse of children that has persisted through several generations. The secrets were not secrets in the sense of being completely hidden from sight, completely denied. Instead, he says, "It was more of a minimization or denial of consequences."

In his forties now, lean and intense, there is anger in his voice as he recalls one time in particular when he complained to his father that his maternal grandfather sexually abused him. "You told me that two weeks ago," his father responded. "It's no big deal. There aren't any scars. Shove off."

On the surface, Kevin grew up in an affluent "Leave It to Beaver" midwestern family. His father was a doctor and his mother was a housewife. "My parents were primarily interested in maintaining this upper middle-class Protestant facade," Kevin comments. He describes his mother as "a perfectionist, an obsessive compulsive, one of those people who vacuums the house twice a day. We had a lawn in an area where it was very hard to grow a lawn. But we had the nicest one in town." His father, meanwhile, "managed to find a meeting to go to every night. He was on every board in town," so he was physically removed from the household for the most part.

In his home, Kevin explains, reality was not so much questioned as it was twisted. "When you're dealing with reality that's continuously distorted, not outright denied, it becomes insidious. It's insidious because in that setting you operate that way too. It's like being in a play. If you spend too much time doing it, then it takes on a reality of its own."

Kevin is the oldest. His two sisters are three and six years younger than he. As he reflects on the way he was brought up, he notes that feelings were never discussed in his home. He remembers a sense of desperation, an inability to express what needed to be expressed. His parents were primarily interested in keeping their children under a tight rein, but since they didn't really believe in spanking, they exerted control in another way.

"Anytime something happened that they didn't like," Kevin explains, "instead of saying 'No, don't do that,' they would attack you personally. In other words, spilling a glass of milk at the table was a moral problem. You didn't do it because you were clumsy. You did it because you wanted to upset your mother. You did it because you were a bad person."

When Kevin was five, his father contracted polio. While he was in the hospital and rehabilitation center, Kevin, his mother, and his sisters went to live with Kevin's maternal grandparents. This is the first memory Kevin has of his grandfather sexually abusing him, although he suspects there may have been earlier incidents. He immediately told his father, who, he says, "told me that I was misinterpreting what was happening." Kevin's family moved back home several months later, but each time his grandfather visited, the abuse recurred.

"When I was seven or eight," Kevin observes, "I had the impression that my grandfather was much wealthier than he actually was." His grandfather, whom he describes as "a pillar of the community, very well connected," served as the chairman of United Way and held a senior position at the major corporation in town. From Kevin's perspective, his grandfather was a powerful figure, in his parents' eyes as well as his own. "I also had the impression, I think correctly, that if I told my parents what he did to me, they'd get very upset with me. I'd already had that experience once, so I figured telling them wouldn't do much good. I had very low expectations of my parents. They really disappointed me. I had told my father once that I didn't want to spend any time with my grandfather, that I didn't want to be around him, and those wishes weren't respected."

When Kevin was fourteen, his grandmother died and his grandfather went on vacation with his family. They went to a summer resort, where Kevin was put in one cabin with his grandfather while the rest of the family settled into a second cabin. Kevin told his parents he didn't want to do this, but they ignored his concerns again, saying that his sisters were growing up and that he was too old to be in with the rest of the family. His grandfather molested him throughout the summer and Kevin kept his mouth shut. He figured that if his parents made him sleep there despite his protests, they knew on some level what was happening and it was acceptable to them.

The following summer his grandfather moved in with the family, and he attempted to continue the abuse. But by this time Kevin had grown. "I was finally physically big enough to stop him." He recalls that his grandfather sulked and continually tried to make trouble for him, "so I told my father what was happening and this time he acted on it. He didn't have any choice. I would have thrown him down the stairs if he'd ignored me."

His father kicked his grandfather out of the house. "My mother got upset. She totally freaked out. She just didn't know how to handle it."

After his grandfather was out, however, Kevin's life deteriorated quickly. "That was the end of the physical abuse," he says, "but I think that's when the psychological abuse from my parents really intensified." Both his mother and father continued to accuse him of making a big deal out of nothing. They were angry at him for causing trouble, angry at him for causing upheaval between them and the grandfather.

Kevin reacted by going into a tailspin. He went from being one of the best students in his class in his freshman year to right at the bottom by the end of his sophomore year.

"The roof caved in," he remembers. "I felt very depressed. My mother was totally hostile." His father offered Kevin no emotional support, but instead prescribed antidepressants for him. "My parents were very concerned about appearances," he reiterates.

Kevin is thoughtful in trying to explain why he managed to do well in school while his grandfather lived with his family and continued to molest him, but then fell apart when his grandfather moved out and the abuse ended. "I have to be careful when I say this," he explains, "but the actual physical act of being sexually abused as a kid isn't a very big deal. The big deal is the way adults react to it. While it's happening, it threatens your sense of self and I suppose one way to cope with that is to do very well in school, which allowed me a certain sense of identity."

Continuing with his roller coaster ride, Kevin began to superachieve, both to compensate for his disastrous sophomore year and to try to regain some control over his life. He took summer courses, worked out with college teams, and in his words, "started conning everyone in sight." He scored spectacularly on the College Board Exams, achieved like crazy, and pulled off an early decision acceptance at an Ivy League school at the end of his junior year. "As long as I was active and focused on a goal like getting into a first-rate school, I didn't have to deal with what had happened at home," he reflects.

According to Kevin, his parents' pattern of ignoring and trivializing his abuse was consistent with the way they treated their children generally.

"My sisters and I were put in the position of being responsible for ourselves at a very early age, well before we should have been," he says. "After my sisters were born, after they stopped nursing and were potty trained, my mother just faded out of the picture."

By default, Kevin assumed a role with his sisters that he says he wasn't ready for. "I tried particularly to protect my younger sister from my mother, from her viciousness," he recalls, "but with my father's total lack of support." He couldn't supply the nurturing his sisters needed, he says, not only because he was a child himself but because "if you've never gotten any of that, you don't know how to give it." But getting out of the house and into college didn't lessen any of Kevin's problems. Partway through his sophomore year (1965–66), bombing began in the north of Vietnam. Like a lot of people of his vintage, he found himself changing.

"I went from being a relatively conservative Republican type to becoming a member of SDS (Students for a

Democratic Society)." He switched his major from premed to political economics. He also started drinking heavily and, like many incest survivors, he began having other problems.

"It wasn't just the alcohol," he says. "My father still had me on medication. It started out with antidepressants, but then I had trouble sleeping, because I had a lot of anxiety about my grandfather coming to me in the night. So my father started prescribing sleeping pills too."

"College," he summarizes, "went very unsmoothly. I was in and out of four different schools and I didn't get my bachelor's degree until I was twenty-eight. I was in a real state of crisis in terms of who I was and what was going on."

During those years, Kevin made several sporadic attempts at therapy, but he says, "I think just about everybody that I spoke with up until I started with my current therapist either accused me of making it up or told me that it wasn't significant." He recalls one psychiatrist who said to him, "Well, you already told me about your grandfather last time. Now let's talk about what's really going on in your life."

When asked if there were any positive aspects to growing up in his family, Kevin grimaces and then says, grudgingly, "Well, there were always plenty of books in the house. But I've really gotten out of touch with the positive stuff because, in terms of all else that happened, it seems so trivial. I suppose it's nicer to be in prison with classical music playing in the background. . . . "

Kevin suspects that incest was nothing new in his family. He thinks his abuse was part of a grander pattern and he believes that his mother may well have been victimized by her father, who was of course the same grandfather who abused him.

"She wasn't a very well-integrated personality," he says, becoming cool and clinical as he describes her. "I would say she had a full blown multiple personality syndrome."

Kevin continues to explain that his mother became very upset when, in his thirties, he told her about his own abuse and the way it had affected him. He notes that his mother was treated over the years by a series of male psychiatrists, for whom Kevin appears to hold little respect.

Kevin assumes that they did not attach much importance to incest, just as the male clinicians he had consulted minimized his own experiences. His mother eventually committed suicide and he thinks it was partly the result of her getting in touch with her own experiences as he told her about his.

In general Kevin does not speak glowingly of those in the helping professions. "People go into the helping fields in many cases because they saw a lot of injustice when they were kids," he says. "But they also tend to be in denial about the most painful parts of it." If they haven't dealt with their own experiences adequately, he reasons, how can they acknowledge the depth of the pain their clients bring to them?

It is clear that Kevin is well-informed and that he has done a great deal of thinking on the subject. While he is able to refer to Freud with facility, he is also able to articulate clearly his own view of why behavioral problems result. He believes that children have a relatively simple sense of justice and that when that sense of justice is violated, difficulties develop.

In the process of coming to terms with what happened to himself as a child, Kevin began attending Parents United, a support group for families in crisis which tries to deal with incest survivors, their parents, and their abusers. The organization, however, puts more emphasis on keeping the family together than Kevin could accept. From there he moved on to Survivors of Incest Anonymous (SIA), which offers support groups which are run by the members themselves, without a trained leader.

"SIA has been very helpful in terms of validating my experience," he says. His particular group is located in Washington, D.C., and he describes its membership as "highly educated, highly successful. We've got a couple of media people and attorneys that are fairly well connected. I mean, you don't walk into this room and start thinking dysfunction."

Unlike some groups, Kevin explains, "We don't allow crosstalk. We think it's difficult enough already for people to talk about this and the spectre of talking and being interrupted is too much."

Picking up on a theme he raised earlier, Kevin acknowledges his belief that "kids can survive all sorts of horrible things" and go on to thrive. The key, he says, is that somewhere in their upbringing "they found an adult figure who provided them with nurturing and support, which I didn't."

Listening to him speak is like listening to a recurring tape, drumming home a relentless chorus. It is like hearing a child's voice saying over and over, "Believe me, believe what I have to say."

Kevin finally settled into a career as a stockbroker after years of searching for a niche. He has no children and has never been married. It has always been difficult for him to form close relationships, a situation which he attributes to his upbringing.

"I couldn't trust my parents to provide even minimal levels of support in anything," he says. "I have a pretty general fear of interaction with other people. It seems strange then that I'm in a sales situation, but it's very structured. I'm in control. I have their money. But I feel very uncomfortable in unstructured situations."

It is only in recent years, as Kevin has established a relationship with a woman who is herself an incest survivor, that he has begun to trust again. He would be quick to admit that he has a long way to go to feeling whole.

As he has begun to heal himself, he has reached out to his sisters. While neither of them has admitted to being sexually abused, he says that "they believe me, but they tend to minimize the impact on their own lives."

"If my parents denied my feelings," he explains, "they were also denying my sisters' feelings." He isn't happy about what happened to him as a child but he recognizes the benefit of acknowledging that something concrete happened to cause his personal distress. He worries that his sisters still believe that whatever troubles they have, the difficulties stem from something intrinsically faulty within themselves, rather than from the circumstances in which they grew up. He points to his younger sister who is currently reliant on antidepressants. Her explanation for her problems is "It's in the genes," a rationale that frustrates Kevin.

"We're talking about somebody who graduated in the top 1% of her class at an Ivy League school, who went on to get her MBA at a top business school, and she's convinced the problem is in her genes." He admits that he once shared her belief, at a time when he relied heavily on lithium, but that he has since discovered that "a vast majority of psychopharmacology is bunk. Obviously there are certain situations that are metabolic, but I think the vast majority is crap. As the bumper sticker says, 'Shit happens.' Well in my family, shit happened, and to the extent that people don't want to deal with it, they try to medicate it away."

Kevin does not ignore the wounds of his past, but he is able to look toward the future with a good dose of optimism. By finding support through incest survivor groups and acknowledging what actually happened in his family, he has enabled himself to move forward. He is convinced that most of the bad experiences he has had in his life resulted from his inability to come to terms with his abuse. "I spent so much time and energy keeping my emotional reaction to it suppressed—in the family I grew up in that kind of expression wasn't legitimate—that I didn't have time for anything else. For the first time in my life I'm starting to trust myself. I guess I've come to terms with the fact that something horrible, something bad did happen, but that life goes on."

Ann

In her late fifties, barely five feet tall, Ann Shore is an accomplished ocean sailor and a successful geologist. Trim and wiry, she wears her penchant for physical and intellectual challenge like a suit of armor. Hidden beneath the toughness is a core of vulnerability, insecurity, and loneliness, rooted in her childhood experiences. Ann was repeatedly molested by her paternal grandfather up until she was seven years old. Like Kevin Rath, she came from a prominent family and her abuser enjoyed a reputation as a powerful pillar of the community. Like Kevin, her secret has undermined her ability to trust and form relationships.

Ann was brought up in the environs of New York City, where her grandfather held a high-ranking position in Mayor Fiorello La Guardia's administration. Immersed in the political scene, he oversaw the development of large scale projects that commanded considerable press attention.

"If you asked anyone at that time what kind of a man my grandfather was," Ann observes, "they would have said he was a wonderful man, kind, sensitive, talented— the whole nine yards. He was as high up as you can go in the Masons and my grandmother was in Eastern Star. They were very sociable and they entertained frequently."

Ann's parents also maintained the facade of an ideal family, but the veneer was thin. Within the house, life was tense and often punctuated by too much drinking. Her mother had a master's degree and her father worked as a successful engineer in a research lab.

"We were considered a solid, upper middle-class family," she says, "but also a kind of snobbish family. My father was a perfectionist and no one could do anything as well as he could. He would tell you that immediately. He was very critical." He was also a heavy drinker, a trait which he inherited from his father. Lowering her voice to an angry hiss, Ann says, "My grandfather was an alcoholic. He was never drunk in public. He was never drunk at work. He started drinking on the Long Island Railway on the way home." When he was drunk and Ann was present, she remembers, "He would come after me no matter what I was doing or who was there."

Ann's grandparents lived in Queens, but they also had a vacation house on Long Island. Her grandmother, whose only child was Ann's father, had long pined for a daughter. So when Ann was born, she immediately began to develop a close relationship, often taking her out to Long Island for the weekend. It was during those visits, Ann thinks, that the abuse began, although she is quick to add that she believes she has repressed much of what happened.

"He'd grab me, put me on his lap, and put his fingers up my vagina. Right in front of everybody—my mother, my grandmother. They would holler at him to stop but usually he wouldn't." While her memories of what happened are vague, Ann has images of blood, and sheets, and being terrified whenever she was left alone with him. "I don't know if he ever penetrated me," she says, "but it wouldn't surprise me because there were plenty of opportunities when I was alone with him."

When Ann was seven, she was raped by a neighborhood boy and she thinks there is a strong connection between this trauma and the early abuse by her grandfather. "Incest begets victimization," she explains. She believes that by ignoring the early abuse that her grandfather inflicted on her and by allowing it to continue, her parents set her up as a future victim.

When a child is taught not to tell, when she is threatened and manipulated into accepting the role of victim in her family, "a mechanism gets activated deep inside which prevents her from protecting herself in a situation where she could be victimized."

One day she went out roller skating with her younger brother and a girlfriend. As they sped around the block she struck out ahead of them. When she was quite far out front, a boy in his late teens and slightly retarded came out of his house and offered her some chocolate cake. She isn't too clear about what happened, but she thinks she took off her skates and went into the house with him. She remembers that he took her up to his bedroom to show her his collection of model airplanes. She recalls blue walls, a globe on the bureau, models everywhere. He took off his clothes, she says, "and asked me to get up on the bed with him. Then he showed me his 'walnuts,' his balls. The next thing I knew he did a real quick flip and put his penis in my mouth. He came, and it was horrible. I don't remember much after that except I was afraid he wasn't going to let me go. I also remember I felt very ashamed, like I'd done something terribly wrong."

She remembers running out of the house, having difficulty opening the front door, running through backyards. She remembers stopping at a huge heap of dirt where she often played king of the mountain with her friends. "His semen was coming down my face and I was afraid that someone would see it," she says quietly. "I picked up dirt and rubbed it all over my face to get the slimy stuff off."

Meanwhile, her girlfriend and brother, who had seen her go into the house where the assault occurred, ran to the girl's house to tell her mother. Her mother called Ann's mother, who was waiting at the door when she got home.

"My mother pulled me inside and told me I was filthy," she remembers, shuddering. "I had the impression, from what she said, that now I was dirty forever, for the rest of my life. She tried to clean me up but it was like, 'I'll do my best but you'll never really be clean again.' " When her father arrived, "he jerked me into the bathroom and pulled my legs apart. I can remember him saying, 'How could you have done this to me?' I was seven. I had done this terrible thing. I believed all this."

Ann's father and grandfather both liked to hunt and there were guns in the house. She recalls thinking her father was going to go get a gun and shoot the boy who molested her, which terrified her because she felt that the boy hadn't done anything wrong and that he shouldn't be hurt. "If anyone should be shot," I thought, "it should be me for doing this horrible thing." She had internalized a message that told her that whatever had happened, it was her fault. Later in the day, after the police had come and gone, her father tied her to a dog line in the yard, where he left her until after dark.

"It dawned on me that my grandfather had been doing these things to me too," she says. "At that point, my whole life changed, how I saw myself. I'd hurt my father. I'd threatened the life of this boy. I'd threatened the relationship between my grandfather and my father. I mean, if my father was going to shoot this boy, what was he going to do to my grandfather?"

It was not until many years later that Ann realized that her father's anger following the rape was a legacy willed to him by his own father, the grandfather who abused her. She is convinced that he too was abused as a child, and that he too was a hostage imprisoned in the thick walls of secrecy constructed to protect the image of the family.

"I thought my father was going to kill me after the rape," she says. "He had had all this stuff bottled up in him for years and what fell on me was all the anger he wanted to put on his father."

Ann testified at the court proceedings that followed and her father managed to pile blame on her even though it was the boy's trial. Her parents have both died since, and to this day Ann cannot remember whether or not the boy was convicted. What Ann does remember is that right after the trial, "that's when I made the decision that I no longer deserved parents, that I no longer had parents, that I was alone in the world, that I was dirty. And that became my secret, and everything I've done ever since has been an effort to conceal that secret."

The trial was in August. In November she turned eight, and in December her grandmother, to whom she was very attached, died. "If anyone had said to me, which no one did, 'It isn't your fault,' I think I would have had a ray of hope," she reflects. "My grandmother was the only one in the whole scenario who might have rescued my self-image at that point, but she had cancer and then she died."

Ann's elementary-school years were lonely and miserable. She started menstruating when she was nine and, she says, "It was horrible. It made me even more sure everyone knew I was dirty and awful."

In high school she excelled academically, but continued to feel inferior and unworthy. She was also terrified of boys and the whole notion of dating. "I was afraid I would fall in love with somebody and that he wouldn't want me," she says. "At the same time, I was afraid that he would want me. I just didn't want to have anything to do with it."

After she finished high school, her parents moved to a rural part of Pennsylvania, where she lived during her college breaks. There was a family a few farms away with three grown boys, whom Ann found ignorant and unpleasant. "The oldest one disgusted me," she recalls, "I don't know why. And yet I ended up doing a roll in the hay with him twice." Thirty years removed from the scene, she thinks she understands what happened.

"My grandfather was repulsive to me, rank and staggering around," she explains. "The boy who had done the rape was repulsive to me physically. So it's like I was attracted sexually to these people who repulsed me. It's almost like I have to be." It's almost, one is tempted to add, as though that is what she feels she deserves.

When she speculates on her choice of geology as a college major, Ann is convinced that "it was back to the womb and all that." She also points out that cave exploration is dirty work, and that "it didn't bother me to walk around covered with mud because I felt like I was covered with mud anyway."

She met her first husband through her caving activities. He was affluent and intelligent, but she wasn't attracted to him physically at all. She knew from the start that the marriage was a mistake. "We went on our honeymoon and I remember feeling like I didn't want him near me. I went through the motions physically but there was nothing there. I didn't love him, ever."

After five years and two children, Ann told him she felt the marriage was failing and that she wanted to leave. He argued against divorce, but shortly afterward she discovered that he was involved with another woman. She revisited all the feelings of worthlessness she had experienced when her father demeaned her following the rape.

Soon after, Ann ended up in a hospital after threatening to kill herself. She poured out all her marital problems to the psychiatrist assigned to her case, never mentioning her childhood experiences. After seven electroshock treatments, she left the hospital feeling that she had "been punished for being unstable and too emotional." Her mother-in-law threatened to take the children away from her, and her own parents reacted to her troubles by telling her to shape up and stop feeling sorry for herself.

"After the shock treatments," she says, "I felt as though this doctor, my parents, my husband, his parents— as though they all recognized what a bad person I was." They all knew her secret, she thought. She was unable to make the connection between her childhood incest experience and her current troubles. She only knew that she was worthless.

She got divorced, got a government job, and set about supporting herself and her two kids. That was in 1964. It was not until 1986, when she got involved in incest therapy, that she began to understand the origins of her difficulties.

"During that twenty-two years," she says, "every day I'd look at this person staring back at me in the mirror and wonder how I could impose her on the world. Twenty-two fucking years, I couldn't look people in the eye."

During this period, she had a series of affairs but none of them led anywhere. "I'd meet somebody," she explains, "and they'd seem very attractive and then I'd get to know them and then they would disgust me physically. That's been the pattern all along."

She married one of these men, "an alcoholic ex-marine with no education," but "it was the same old story." The marriage lasted only two years.

At that point she decided to concentrate on her career. She returned to graduate school, published several papers, and began to develop a reputation in her field.

In 1980, a turning point occurred. "I met this guy," she says, "and for the first time I really fell in love. I let Adam get closer to me than anyone else, but the closer he got the more things about him disgusted me." As problems further developed, Adam told her that he suspected she had never dealt thoroughly with the rape incident. Frantic to save the relationship, which had begun to flounder as she launched her familiar pattern of disgust and distancing, Ann called a rape crisis center and arranged an appointment.

The counselor who saw her quickly identified her as an incest survivor and placed her in an incest survivors' therapy group. She was skeptical, but she started to attend the meetings.

"I was fully in denial," she observes. "I went every week and heard these women talk about being raped by their fathers. I knew I'd been raped, but I didn't feel like I was one of them." After all, she had been raped by a stranger, she reasoned. But several weeks later, changes began.

Driving to Annapolis one evening where she and Adam spent their weekends on a boat, she started feeling disgust toward Adam and apprehension about the evening ahead.

Later, as they were getting ready to go to bed, Adam pulled her down on his lap, "just like my grandfather used to do," she recalls. "Something inside me snapped and I started to cry as I had never done before. The tears came from the depths of me and it was uncontrollable. My mother had taught me that I could and should control all of my reactions all the time, that I was responsible for them. But this was uncontrollable."

She began to realize what had happened. By allowing Adam to get so close to her, she had broken through a barrier she had constructed years back when she decided she was unworthy of having parents. She had begun to trust. When Adam wanted to initiate sex, pulling her playfully onto his lap, she wanted to say 'No,' but she wasn't able to.

"This is the horrible part about incest," she says. "You want to say 'No,' but you're afraid you'll lose the protection of the person, or you'll get killed, or lose your security."

At that point Ann realized that the counselor who labeled her an incest survivor was absolutely correct, that everything the other women in the group were talking about was true of her as well.

"I finally identified my grandfather as the perpetrator," she remembers. "I couldn't understand why I was feeling all this disgust for this guy I loved. Then I finally put together that my grandfather was repulsive to me and yet as a child I was expected to do these sexual things with him. I took Adam out of that image and put my grandfather in his place and it felt right. And I realized that all of the feelings of disgust I had for Adam, I was transferring from my grandfather."

As Ann reflects back on her own history, she is firm in her conviction that no matter how dreadful her grandfather's abuse, her life could have been immeasurably sweeter if her parents had acknowledged and dealt with what happened rather than doing their best to hide it away. She shares with Kevin Rath the belief that parents can help their children heal, if they choose to use their power and authority to support rather than undermine their children's perception of the world. In Kevin's case his parents blatantly ignored his requests for protection. Ann's situation was cloudier. Her parents "hollered at my grandfather to stop doing these things to me," she remembers, but "I don't think anyone really tried to prevent him from getting to me."

As she reflects on her family and the way it functioned, Ann realizes that there was enormous respect for her grandfather and a collective obligation to protect his public persona. "He had a lot of power in the family," she says, "and I think it got used against me. In a sense, I was a sacrifice. I was just a twerp who was stuck in this muck and no one could help me because if the secret got out, his image would be damaged."

While her career and her passion for ocean sailing provide her with considerable fulfillment today, Ann is quick to admit that there is a deep void in her life. Her relationship with Adam was not strong enough to endure the emotional roller coaster that she boarded as she began the long journey back to the past to confront the horrors of her childhood, and the two soon separated.

At age fifty-seven, one might ask, why does she need to continue to pursue the past? It is a question she can answer with clarity. "It would be wonderful," she says, "to have a good, loving relationship with a man before I die." She is determined to unshackle herself from the fear and mistrust that have wedged themselves into her very being as a result of her family secret.

Maggie

Like Kevin and Ann, Maggie Harvey's family maintained a facade of respectability. "We were like a picturebook family," she comments. "We did a lot together, going to museums and farms and antique exhibits. We spent a lot of time with my mother's family, always taking over a turkey for Sunday dinner." It is hard to reconcile this image with the knowledge that Maggie was molested by family members from the time she was an infant up until she was twelve years old. She was sexually abused by her father, her mother, and her grandfather.

"My father molested me only three times that I know of, but they were all very violent acts," she says, almost apologetically, as though to indicate she knows others have endured far more. Like Ann, her experiences catapulted her into the role of victim, making her vulnerable to outsiders. When she was seven she was molested by two adolescent boys. She remembered almost nothing of these incidents until after she had children of her own.

Maggie, who worked as a pediatric nursing supervisor at a major teaching hospital, married Steve in 1971. Both in their early twenties, they recognized that they had some conflicts to work out regarding whether and when to have children.

"I had a strong biological drive toward having kids," explains Maggie, the oldest in a family that included three brothers and a sister, "but I also had a sense that this could be very dangerous."

Steve too had ambivalent feelings. He wanted children, but he had little interest in infants. Caught up in pursuing their careers, they debated the question of parenthood throughout the early years of their marriage without reaching resolution.

In 1976 Maggie's brother Owen came out of the closet. Owen is one year her junior and the sibling to whom she felt the most connection. He told the family he was gay and that he was going to move from their conservative East Coast community to San Francisco to make a life for himself.

While Maggie had never suspected his secret, it didn't surpise her. She did not find it difficult to accept Owen's disclosure, and she continued to talk with him regularly on the phone. At the same time, her own life cracked wide open. After years of ambivalence, she decided she had to have a baby right away. She also realized that she felt responsible for Owen's being gay, although she didn't know why. It was not until several years later that she was able to make sense of her feelings.

Frightened and confused, she began seeing a therapist. In the course of her treatment, she remembered an incident that occurred when she was six and Owen was five.

"My father sodomized the two of us together," she says softly, "and by what he said, he made me feel responsible for my brother getting molested."

Owen, who recently died of AIDS, was "kind of a quiet kid, and gentle, but he was always happy and twinkly and he had a sense of fun."

On that day of abuse, Maggie saw her brother change in front of her eyes. After it happened, she remembers looking at him as he came out of the room in his pajamas. "He looked like somebody had taken everything out of him. His whole face, it was just absolutely like a mask, and he looked at me, and he looked so humiliated and betrayed. I'll never forget that as long as I live."

Maggie's therapist never used the word "incest" when they talked about this incident, which came to Maggie in a dream that left her gasping for breath. And Maggie says that when she left therapy she still didn't understand where her problems were rooted.

"It would have been more helpful if she had labeled what happened," she says. "If she had said, 'That's incest, and it's wrong.' Then I would have had a word. I could have gone and looked it up in the dictionary. It was like being an alcoholic and not knowing what alcohol is called."

Yet Maggie is firm in her conviction that the sessions were a useful beginning because, she says, "I think I started to realize that I could talk to people about things, that I could get people to listen to me, that this wasn't crazy, that these were real concerns, and that I could change."

Before Owen left for the West Coast he tried to talk to Maggie about their childhood and the abuse they endured. Maggie, however, was not receptive. "He seemed to be trying to tell me that there were times when getting sex as a child was okay because it was a form of love. Well, using children for sex isn't love. It's manipulation. I just said, 'That's not right—I won't discuss this.'

"But when I look back I think what he was trying to do was to open it up and have me tell him that what had happened was not his fault. I just couldn't discuss the subject then, especially since there was a difference in how we thought about it. I never brought it up again and he never did either, and that's really too bad."

During this time, Maggie and her husband tried to conceive a child, but with no luck. After numerous tests Maggie was told that she had severe endometriosis and that it was unlikely she would ever become pregnant. She left therapy after a year and a half, having made the decision to adopt.

Two years later, in 1980, the Harveys flew to Mexico to pick up their newborn son. Within weeks Maggie discovered she was pregnant. Eight months after she brought her adoptive son Scott home, her daughter Irene was born.

Maggie found herself overwhelmed. Depressed and unable to handle her own feelings, she lashed out at her babies. She knew that her impatience and temper outbursts were detrimental to her kids but she attributed her behavior at first to the stress involved in mothering two infants.

"When I walked in the door with the first baby, I felt all my defenses crumble," she recalls. "I don't know how to describe what happened, but I knew I was in a lot of trouble."

With the arrival of her daughter, her difficulties escalated drastically. "At times I was abusive, no question about that," she says. "I couldn't tolerate their crying at all. I had expected myself to be a patient, loving mother but I was emotionally out of control. I didn't realize until much later that what I was doing was screaming and crying when anything reminded me of my own abuse."

Convinced that she could not take care of her children, Maggie solved her problem by sending them to daycare even though she was at home. Her previous therapist had passed away and she began to see a series of new ones, but she had not found anyone with whom she was completely comfortable.

"I was in therapy all this time," she comments, "but I still didn't know what the issue was. I didn't have a name for what it was so it was hard for people to be able to help me. That's what secrets do. You don't even have the words to talk about what it is that's happening." During this time, she came across a brochure that talked about rape victims. She read the list of symptoms and thought, "That sounds like me, but I haven't been raped." Desperate for relief from the anxiety, uncontrollable crying, and breathing difficulties that plagued her, she called the hotline. "I said, 'I haven't been raped but I need to talk to you anyway,' And they were great. They saved my life, just listening to me. I'll bet I called them every day for a year."

Eventually Maggie settled into a four-year-long relationship with a therapist who provided the direction and sense of security she needed in order to unearth her buried memories. She believes now that she has recalled most of the abusive incidents that happened to her as a child, and as horrible and painful as the process of retrieving those memories has been, she is completely convinced that her life is immensely better for having been through it.

"You're disempowered when you don't know what's causing your distress," she explains. "For years I had had this jigsaw puzzle on top of my table, trying to put it together. Looking for a corner here, an edge piece there. It was like, 'What the hell is this thing?' " When her memories flooded back, it was as though the whole picture came together. She understood clearly what had happened to her and how it had affected her ability to nurture her own children.

Although it had been years since she first remembered the incident when her father molested her and Owen together, she now recalled the details of what had happened far more clearly, putting it into perspective.

Right after the incident, she explains, her father dressed the two of them up and took them to church. "He took us every day for two weeks," she says. "One morning on our way there, I spoke up to him and said, 'You know, Dad, what you did to us the other night was wrong.' He turned on me and said we were bad, dirty children."

This incident had happened while her mother was in the hospital having a baby. When her mother got home, she was so busy that Maggie found her unapproachable.

Sometime later she mustered the courage to tell her mother what her father had done. "That's when she raped me with her fingers," she says. "She lost it. Stuck her fingers up my vagina. Went into a rage. 'Don't you dare ever say anything like that!' " Her mother's reaction confirmed her sense that she was alone, that speaking up would only endanger her already precarious position in the family.

When asked if there was anyone who offered her a sense of security as a child, Maggie responded that she always felt safe with her maternal grandfather. When she was seven, however, she went on an errand with him to a neighbor's house. Her grandfather went inside "to do business over the kitchen table," Maggie recalls, leaving her in the yard to play with the neighbors' teenage boys.

"They lured me into the woods, saying they had seen a rabbit, and they molested me," she remembers. "When my grandfather came out, he could see that I was all covered with scratches and obviously something was very wrong." She doesn't remember talking about what had happened but she does recall that her grandfather must have known because "he made it very clear to me that what the boys had done was wrong." He took her back to his house where he and Maggie's grandmother bathed her and cleaned the scratches with Witch Hazel.

"I remember them talking to each other," she says, and they decided that they wouldn't tell my parents what happened because my parents would think that they hadn't protected me properly." From their conversation, Maggie surmised that she too should remain silent. If she told her parents, she would be betraying her grandparents. Right then, another secret was created.

Sadly for Maggie, her loyalty to her grandfather was not reciprocated. When she was twelve, he molested her. "My grandfather never did that to me until he was virtually senile," she says. "I was really fond of him, so when he did, it seemed like a terrible betrayal, like, 'Oh, you too?' "

Today, seven years after most of her memories returned, Maggie actively continues to seek out assistance so that she will continue to heal. She and her husband are no longer together, their marriage unable to sustain the strain of her battle to come to terms with her childhood. Maggie currently attends a support group of incest survivors which gives her considerable comfort.

"When you have to keep these things secret, it corrodes your insides," she says. "You're isolated. It splits you off from everybody. In the group, you start hearing people say, 'That happened to you? It happened to me too.' Then you realize you aren't crazy because other people have had the same experiences, often under the same circumstances. You go from being an isolated child who's split off because she blames herself for what happened to being part of a roomful of people saying, 'That happened to me too.' "

What Maggie sees when she looks back on her childhood and the way her family functioned is "a lot of totally unnecessary suffering." What she has learned, she says, is that any problem can be faced when it is out in the open.

"That I had to go through all of this is bad enough," Maggie reflects, "but that my children, the two little ones whom I cherish most, have had to relive it with me, I'll never get over that. I think they deserve to have a whole mother."

As part of her effort to give them just that, with the help of a therapist she has told her children, now nine and ten years, that she was sexually abused as a child. By breaking her secret and confronting its aftermath, Maggie has been able to reach out for the professional assistance her children need to help them to acknowledge their own feelings and to come to grips with the way their mother's experience affects them.

"Secrets are so harmful because they lock you in yourself," she explains. "If only someone had said to me when I was a child, 'That shouldn't have happened, and it's not your fault, and we're going to do such and such to make sure it never happens again,' " she sighs, "I think it would have made a tremendous difference."

8

Making Peace with Our Secrets

I N the preceeding chapters I have described secrets that revolve around the identity of parents and siblings. I have touched too on secrets formed to conceal sexual abuse, sexual identity, mental illness, alcoholism, and infractions of the law. In the course of researching this book, many people have generously shared their stories. While some were at first reluctant, most warmed to the challenge once they had begun. Although no easy mission for them, recounting their experiences often became illuminating. By telling their stories, most were able to gain a broader perspective on what had happened and what it means to them in the present. By articulating their stories and reflecting on them, many felt as though they had stitched together images and feelings that stretched across years. It seems the storytellers were able to assimilate their experiences by seeing them as a whole.

While the stories presented in earlier chapters are representative of the kinds of issues that give rise to family secrets, there are many other stories too. When I started talking to people about my interest in exploring the use of secrecy in families, almost inevitably they had a story of their own to tell or knew of someone else who did. I cannot recall how often my description of this book was greeted with the statement, "Every family has secrets." And, indeed, it appears they do.

One woman told me how her family—a respectable lawyer in a small Midwestern town, his wife, and two daughters—spent some of their vacations in a nudist camp. The children were in on the secret, and the children helped to keep the secret from getting out and damaging their father's law practice.

"It just made sense," she told me. "If my parents had left us home and lied to us about where they were going and if I had found out, I think I would have considered it a lack of trust, but I was brought up in a family where there was a lot of trust. If anything, it brought our family closer. I was kind of proud that I came from a family that had the guts to be a little different."

A woman friend in her thirties told me that her father's secret was that he had a sister who had a serious accident when she was three and who died when she was a teenager. My friend didn't learn about the existence of this person, who would have been her aunt, until she was nearly grown up. "When I was about sixteen," she says, "my father took me out to dinner at a fancy restaurant and kind of bluntly said, 'I just wanted to tell you that I had a sister and that she fell down the stairs and suffered severe brain problems. She died when she was eighteen.' Then it was sort of like, 'How's your steak?' And we never talked about it again."

One man told me that when he thinks of secrecy in his family he thinks of his maternal grandparents and the way their behavior affected his own mother. His mother's secret was that her parents were separated most of the time that she was growing up. "I don't know if my mother kept this as a conscious secret," he says, "but I don't think I really knew what the circumstances were until I was a teenager. And at that time, learning about the separation made sense of a lot of memories and things she had told my brother and me that didn't make sense before—like taxi stories."

When his mother reminisces about her childhood, she often talks of driving through Manhattan in a taxicab with her younger brother. She talks about how magical those rides were and how she wanted them to last forever. "I never realized where that intensity sprang from," this man observes, "until I found out that these were the only opportunities the two kids had to see their father, going to spend a weekend or an afternoon with him." He wonders if his mother's memory of wanting the taxicab rides to go on forever might also represent her wish to remain in a sort of limbo between her parents, where she didn't have to be a proxy in their disputes.

While I do not hold to the notion that parents should share all with their children in all cases, the stories I have heard convince me that we often use our desire to protect and shield our children from pain as an excuse that lets us avoid experiencing that pain ourselves. Telling secrets, setting the record straight, involves stirring up troublesome memories and feelings and risking an onslaught of difficult emotions in both ourselves and our families. It needs to be done with sensitivity, but in most cases it does need to be done.

Before disclosing a secret, however, we need to explore our own motivation. Are we telling the secret because we want to manipulate our children into pitying us, into siding against their other parent, into admiring or fearing us? Or are we sharing the information because we think it will help our children to understand the context of their upbringing? Will the story help them to make sense of their own lives and of the stress, disappointments, and ambiguities that they sense in the family?

Secrets divide us into insiders and outsiders, but they do more than that. The number and types of secrets we keep from one another define our relationships. They touch on how much we trust and distrust each other, how we gauge each other in terms of strength or weakness. Secrets can also help us to define ourselves. What is it about our history that is so painful, so threatening, so shameful, that we need to conceal it? Keeping secrets can create an atmosphere of tension, which is relieved when family members have the opportunity to confront the information and openly air their feelings about it. Just as keeping secrets can be divisive, sharing them can build equality, respect, and trust between members of a family.

In telling our secrets, we need to be mindful of balance. We need to be wary of telling our children too little in the guise of protecting them, because by protecting them we also exclude and isolate them, leaving them with no outlet for their feelings and no source of comfort and support in their sadness or confusion. On the other hand, when we overconfide in our children, we catapult them prematurely into adulthood, into the role of caretaker, without giving them the opportunity to experience the rebellion and stages of separation that are part of healthy growth. This sometimes happens when one parent uses a child as a buffer against the other. We have to be careful then not use the revelation of a secret as a weapon in a family dispute.

We form secrets to protect our reputations and those of our relatives, to protect our image of ourselves in the eyes of our children and of the greater community. Sometimes we keep secrets because we fear our children will love us less if they discover our mistakes. As a result, they learn to keep their troubles from us, to mimic our behavior by storing away shameful incidents, thus depriving themselves of our help when they need it. When we give our children access to our faults and failures, as well as to our attributes and successes, we give them the opportunity to know us clear through to the bone. In accepting and revealing ourselves, we give our children permission to do the same for themselves.

When I began to research this book, I believed I would be able to provide specific guidelines instructing parents how and when and in exactly what words to tell their secrets. In the course of the interviews I have conducted and the many conversations I've had about secrecy, I've come to reject that premise. The right time, the right tone, and the right words are not rigid. Indeed, the word "right" is really irrelevant. What is important is to convey the information accurately and compassionately, encouraging the child to voice his or her own feelings and to ask questions, not only at the moment, but in the future, as the child has time to absorb and think about the information that has been shared.

Often it is helpful to anticipate questions that might be asked of us so that we have a chance to think through our answers. Saying "I don't know," when that's the truth, is often the wisest response. If we answer questions in the simplest possible terms as they arise, the secret may unfold graciously as the child is intellectually and emotionally ready to accept it. As the child matures and gains more experience in the world, his or her questions will become more sophisticated and thoughtful, and so too should our answers.

When we share secrets with our children, we help them define who we are and, by extension, where they come from. Children show a remarkable capacity for forgiveness when they are told the truth, unattractive and painful though it may be. When kids learn secrets inadvertently, we erode their trust in us and in others. Keeping a secret sometimes is saying, "You can't handle it, you're not smart enough, you're not tough enough." Keeping a secret is also saying, "Mistakes need to be hidden; people who make mistakes are bad and shameful."

Often we avoid breaking a secret because we don't know how to do it. If I have learned one vital lesson from my research, it is that doing it at all is what is important. We may stammer, we may cry, we may not present the story as smoothly as we would like. What matters most is that we make our best effort. Because only when the revelation has been made can the conversation begin. Only when the bridge has been built can we reach across the chasm and begin to make sense of our experience.